BY NICHOLAS MURRAY BUTLER

The Effect of the War of 1812 Upon the Consolidation of the Union—Johns Hopkins University Press, 1887—30 pp.

The Meaning of Education: Contributions to a Philosophy of Education—Charles Scribner's Sons, 1915 (First Edition, The Macmillan Co., 1898)—xiii + 385 pp.

True and False Democracy—Charles Scribner's Sons, 1915 (First Edition, The Macmillan Co., 1907)—xii + 111 pp.

The American As He Is—Charles Scribner's Sons, 1915 (First Edition, The Macmillan Co., 1908)—x + 104 pp.   New Edition, 1937.

Philosophy: An Essay in Definition—Columbia University Press, 1911—vii + 51 pp.

Why Should We Change Our Form of Government? Studies in Practical Politics—Charles Scribner's Sons, 1912—xvi + 159 pp.

The International Mind: An Argument for the Judicial Settlement of International Disputes—Charles Scribner's Sons, 1913—xii + 121 pp.

The Basis of Durable Peace: Papers Written at the Invitation of "The New York Times" by Cosmos—Charles Scribner's Sons, 1917—ix + 144 pp.

A World in Ferment: Interpretations of the War for a New World—Charles Scribner's Sons, 1917—viii + 254 pp.

Is America Worth Saving?: Studies in National Problems and Party Policies—Charles Scribner's Sons, 1920—xiii + 398 pp.

Scholarship and Service: The Policies and Ideals of a National University in a Modern Democracy—Charles Scribner's Sons, 1921—xii + 399 pp.

Building the American Nation: An Essay of Interpretation—Charles Scribner's Sons, 1923—xviii + 375 pp.

The Faith of a Liberal: Essays and Addresses on Political Principles and Public Policies—Charles Scribner's Sons, 1924—xiii + 369 pp.

The Path to Peace: Essays and Addresses on Peace and Its Making—Charles Scribner's Sons, 1930—xiii + 320 pp.

Looking Forward: What Will the American People Do About It?: Essays and Addresses on Matters National and International—Charles Scribner's Sons, 1932—xiv + 402 pp.

Between Two Worlds: Interpretations of the Age in Which We Live—Charles Scribner's Sons, 1934—xvi + 450 pp.

The Family of Nations: Its Need and Its Problems—Charles Scribner's Sons, 1938—xiii + 400 pp.

Across the Busy Years—Charles Scribner's Sons
Vol. I—xii + 451 pp., 1939.
Vol. II—xii + 472 pp., 1940.

Why War?—Charles Scribner's Sons, 1940—xii + 323 pp.

Liberty — Equality — Fraternity—Charles Scribner's Sons, 1942—xiv + 240 pp.

LIBERTY—EQUALITY—FRATERNITY

ESSAYS AND ADDRESSES

ON THE

PROBLEMS OF TODAY AND TOMORROW

Liberty — Equality — Fraternity

ESSAYS AND ADDRESSES

ON THE

PROBLEMS OF TODAY AND TOMORROW

BY

NICHOLAS MURRAY BUTLER

President of Columbia University
President of the Carnegie Endowment for International Peace
Member of the American Academy of Arts and Letters
Membre de l'Institut de France

NEW YORK

CHARLES SCRIBNER'S SONS

1942

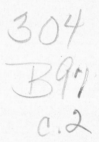

TO THOSE WHO IN ANY LAND
CAN AND DO LOOK FORWARD
WITH FAITH AND WITH COURAGE

CONTENTS

INTRODUCTION

The world chaos which now confronts mankind needs no new description and requires no new emphasis. Finally, and by reason of unparalleled acts of cruelty and governmental immorality, public opinion in the democracies which still survive has been completely aroused. It is now plain that, whatever may appear on the surface, the underlying struggle is between a world whose economic, social and political systems are unified and held in control by armed force, and a world of free, independent and self-governing nations, each of which, whether great or small, is protected in its freedom by rules of international law and international morality, upheld by a world organization with an international police force. In other words, the contest is between an incredible despotism and the type of liberty and free organization contemplated by the resolution unanimously adopted by the Congress of the United States and signed by President Taft in June, 1910. The first and predominant policy of the democracies must be to win the brutal and murderous war into which, wholly against their will, they have been driven. For the democracies, this is a war of self-defense. Everything in which they believe and for which they have gained so much during the past three hundred years is now at stake.

When victory comes, be it soon or late, the democracies must be prepared to act with promptness, foresight and complete understanding to do all in their power to make any repetition of this colossal world disturbance impossible under any conditions. This means that they must understand what Liberty and what Democracy really mean. They must grasp the fact that these are not mere words. They are the names and symbols of ideas and ideals. Agreement as to their meaning must be so universal among the democratic peoples that the application of these ideas and ideals can go forward with all reasonable speed and safety.

This in turn means that public opinion in the democracies must be educated to the fullest possible understanding of these ideas and their problems. Public opinion must be prepared not only to stir and to stimulate governments, but to guide those governments in shaping a world organization upon such new application of the federal principle as will, in effect, do for the whole world what the Constitution of the United States and the organization of the British Commonwealth of Nations have been able to do so successfully for the English-speaking peoples.

The time has passed for repeating the old and meaningless slogans of national isolation, national sovereignty and of every nation minding its own business. Such national isolation as existed before time and distance were destroyed by electric power and by mechanical device, has wholly disappeared. The great oceans and the air, which were supposed to hold nations apart and to isolate them from each other, have proved to be the best-paved roads in the world.

Nor is there now any significance in the term national sovereignty. No nation is sovereign. The moral law rules nations as well as individuals, and it is to the moral law that obedience must be shown in national policies and in international relationships.

This fact makes it impossible for a modern nation to assert that it is minding its own business when it fails to take cognizance of cruel and criminal acts by other nations before its very eyes. One can hardly be said to be minding his own business when he fails to assist in quenching a fire in a house which he does not own or occupy, or in checking an assault made in his presence on a man or a woman who does not happen to be his relative. This form of nonsense, which has been loudly repeated from time to time in these United States, must now be ended.

Given acceptance of the rule of moral law and moral principle, and given also a truly reflective knowledge of what is going on in the world and of why it is going on, public opinion in the remaining democracies can not only win this world war, but when it is won can lay the foundations for long-time, perhaps even permanent, prosperity and peace.

NICHOLAS MURRAY BUTLER

COLUMBIA UNIVERSITY
  IN THE CITY OF NEW YORK
    April 2, 1942

I

LIBERTY EQUALITY FRATERNITY

An address delivered
at the Parrish Memorial Art Museum
Southampton, Long Island
August 31, 1941

LIBERTY EQUALITY FRATERNITY

What has happened? This question is being pressed throughout the world by a startled and perplexed generation. It is asked not only by philosophers and intellectual leaders, but by millions of men and women of every sort and type who are not scholars and who make no claim to scholarship. It is being asked in every land. Interest in this question is profound, alike in Europe, in Asia, in Africa and in the Americas.

It was no less an authority than Gibbon who said of Tacitus that he was the first of historians who applied the science of philosophy to the study of facts.[1] The time has come to do whatever may lie in our power to learn the lessons taught by Tacitus and by Gibbon. The one outstanding philosopher in the world of today, the Italian Benedetto Croce, has just now published a volume of absorbing interest which offers the best possible approach to an understanding of what is really going on in this twentieth-century world.[2] A reading of this remarkable book will go far toward giving to men and women of today an insight into the forces which are at work in the world and a comprehension of their significance and of how, if at all, they may be controlled.

[1]Gibbon, Edward, *History of the Decline and Fall of the Roman Empire*. (London: Methuen and Company, 1896). Volume I, p. 121.
[2]Croce, Benedetto, *History as the Story of Liberty*. (New York: Norton and Company, 1941).

3

The shock of these happenings has been so great that vast numbers have been stunned by it. What they had supposed to be well-founded faith in controlling principles of thought and of morals, of social, of economic and of political organization, is treated with disdain and contempt. The rule of reason has been displaced by that of cruel and merciless brute force, while the precepts of morals and the ideals of religious faith are disregarded entirely. The great religions of the world are despised and assailed for the reason that they, each and all, call for faith in a God, an overruling Providence, who does not happen to come under the jurisdiction of any present-day despot, but must, if He exists at all, be that despot's rival and competitor. Moreover, the ruling agency of these relentless despots is irrational and violent emotion. It uses as its battle-cry: "We do not know where we are going—come along!" It has been clever enough to take possession of ardent and ambitious youth by its absolute control of the schools and the process of education and by the elimination of a score of the world's historic universities with that freedom of thought and of expression which is now more than two hundred years old. By powerful and most ingenious military organization and equipment these new animal forces have conquered one civilized and free people after another. These conquered peoples, being deprived of the instruments of war and of the capacity to produce them, are helpless to resist the armed forces which serve not only as their police, but as their rulers, both local and national. In short, we are learning how easy it may be to conquer and to rule the world if religion and morals are thrown to the winds, and if the whole of the world's instrumentalities in the making and use of armed force are confined to the governments of the ruling despots.

Had it been predicted that the rapid development of liberal thought and policy which became so obvious in the seventeenth century, which reached its age of enlightenment in the eighteenth and which could record the achievements of the English, the American and the French revolutions, would be followed in another century or two by the appalling reaction which now everywhere confronts us, the prophet would have found himself without believers and without honor in his own country. Of all the manifestations of this reaction, none has been more startling or more ominous than the formal renunciation and denunciation of that truly great motto, LIBERTÉ ÉGALITÉ FRATERNITÉ, by those who for the time being are in position to speak for the French people. One might think that it would have seemed sufficient to offer new interpretation to these words, but to disavow them completely and to have them removed from the hundreds of public buildings on which they had so long been carved, simply passes comprehension. Incidentally, it reveals an obvious lack of a sense of humor.

What is it which has made possible and caused these literally preposterous acts? The only answer can be that they are the result of acceptance, willing or unwilling, of a doctrine of social organization which would substitute permanent class groups and distinctions for that form of free and orderly social, economic and political organization which represents and reflects the spirit and the ideals of a true liberalism. Since it is plainly impossible to go back, either in France or elsewhere, to a ruling class of landowners or inherited nobility, this can only mean the intention to set up by force a state of fixed and permanent economic, social and political classes to displace a state of free men to whom every opportunity for improvement, for distinction and for service would be open. It is grotesque to call this a New Order. In all essentials it is one of the oldest orders that human history records. This indicates, once more, how important it is for those who would guide their fellow men, to be in possession both of a map and a compass.

In their present form, these doctrines reflect and would apply the teachings which were pressed upon the world nearly a century ago by Karl Marx and the group of which he was a ruling member. One has only to read the story of the life of Marx at Cologne, in Paris, in Brussels and in London to see to how great an extent what he said and wrote was the outcome of that spirit of envy, hatred and malice by which he was surrounded throughout his life. Indeed, all attempts and plans to suppress or to limit individual accomplishment on other than moral grounds have this same foundation. It may be Communism, it may be Nazism or it may be the less extreme Fascism, but each and all reflect and embody that spirit of envy which is the unworthy result of observing the rise in the world of others than one's self.

Of course, these attempts at restriction, compulsion and despotism are all advanced on grounds of public interest and public advantage. It is the common man, so-called, the ordinary man, who is to be protected by them. The fact is, however, that what is being attempted would have just the opposite effect. It would sentence the individual, however talented, however ambitious or however competent, to remain in the group or class into which he was born. It would stop all true progress and substitute mechanical mass production for individual originality, achievement and high human service.

It is moral principles and moral ideals, and those alone, by which an individual's work in the world should be limited. Any limitation imposed by sheer force without regard to moral principles is reactionary in the extreme, as well as destructive of all excellence. Instead of being in the interest of the great mass of the people, it is distinctly and violently against that interest. It would destroy the very foundations upon which free institutions rest and would substitute some one of the many forms of despotism for that free government through public opinion which we have come to know as democracy. Under such a system of social, economic and political organization and government, Liberty, Equality and Fraternity would all disappear. When Voltaire wrote that "It is inevitable that mankind should be divided into two classes with many subdivisions—the oppressors and the oppressed," he turned his back upon the rule of moral principle and assumed a world where selfishness and force alone were in control.

Croce points out that the German philosopher Hegel was the author of the famous statement that history is the history of Liberty.[3] The story is a long and fascinating one, since it reveals the power of the wish for

[3] *Op. cit.*, p. 59.

Liberty and the skill with which, in one form or another, the rule of Liberty was strengthened through the centuries. It makes it plain that, as was said by Montesquieu, "Liberty does not consist in doing what one pleases . . . Liberty can only consist in being able to do what one ought to do." This great struggle reached its victorious climax as the eighteenth century drew to its close, when the people of what was to become the United States of America formulated the Bill of Rights and incorporated it in the newly adopted Federal Constitution, and when shortly thereafter the French people, acting through their Constituent Assembly at Versailles in 1789, drew up as their guiding principles the Declaration of the Rights of Man. The English people had begun still earlier, although with less formality, to write modern history in this field of thought and action.

Today probably no word, unless it be Democracy, is used so carelessly and often with so little understanding, as the word Liberty. It is fundamental that Liberty is not a grant by government, but that government is a delegation of power by people who have Liberty, and that this government must always be subject to their control. It is the chief business of a free people, and their greatest responsibility, to see to it that the government which they have set up does not, under one pretense or another, invade the reserved field of Liberty and restrict it in a manner which the free people themselves have never authorized or contemplated. In a democracy the state and government are wholly distinct. The state is the field of reserved Liberty plus the field of government. State and government can be identical only when Liberty has wholly disappeared. The constant struggle of those who are, consciously or unconsciously, enemies of Liberty is to increase, even to multiply, the function and authority of government. Education, on the other hand, is the instrumentality by which the people are to be taught and trained to use so wisely their opportunities in the field of Liberty that the public interest is constantly carried forward constructively and helpfully, without inviting or permitting government to invade the field of reserved Liberty. The notion that all governments in what we call democracies are truly representative of the whole people and that their every act is to be accepted by the people without discussion, is most unreasonable. Theoretically, in a democratically organized state, government represents the will of the majority of the people, but, in fact, as very little study of election statistics will show, what government too often represents is really the influence of small, well-organized, persistent and frequently self-seeking minority groups. The political history of the American people abounds in illustrations of this fact. Some of them are familiar, but many of them, having taken place beneath the surface, have been known but to the few. Actually, in our federal system of government the one and only representative of the whole people and the only one chosen by them is the President of the United States. Senators chosen from and by the several states and representatives in Congress chosen from and by the various congressional districts are in many cases brought forward by very small but stubborn and ambitious groups, and carried through to election by a vote of only some 10 per cent to 30 per cent of the entire possible vote of the state or district which they then claim to represent. This is one reason why calm, dispassionate and non-partisan consideration of problems of outstanding public interest and importance is so often impossible, since the attention of members of the federal legislature is almost wholly fixed on those matters which are urged upon them persistently —and often with threats—by highly organized and self-seeking minorities. It is this habit which throws light on what Jefferson called "the morbid rage of debate."

The chief problem which confronts the lover of Liberty is the preservation of that Liberty. It faces two dangers—on the one hand, regimentation and despotism, and on the other hand, license. Free men have long since drawn a clear line between Liberty and license. It was Burke who asked, "What is liberty without wisdom and without virtue? It is the greatest of all possible evils." What he meant was that without those two limitations Liberty becomes license.

The Sixth, Seventh, Eighth and Ninth Commandments which Moses brought down from Mount Sinai were written into the moral law and then into the statute law of one people after another. Violation of any one of these four Commandments is not an act of Liberty, but of license, and this violation has long since been made a crime, punishable as such. There are many other misuses of Liberty which have not risen to the height of being defined as criminal, but which are unreasonable, improper and even dangerous acts of license.

The line between Liberty and license can never be drawn with mathematical accuracy, but the wise man instinctively knows where that line is. Unbalanced and

confused imaginations lose sight of any distinction whatever between Liberty and license. There are organizations for the defense of civil liberty whose energies and
exhortations are often directed to the defense of what
are plainly un-civil liberties, namely license. Those who
are victims of such states of mind become not only a
public nuisance, but often a public danger. Moreover,
they bring about undeserved criticisms of Liberty itself,
and are pointed to by those who prefer despotism as
evidence of the folly of trying to establish and preserve
Liberty for mankind in general. Probably Liberty has
no more powerful enemy than license. Men are often
deceived by what is license, when they would be quick
to understand and to resent an attack on Liberty by
despotism. In the present-day economic organization
of the world, it is of vital importance that the free man
preserve his freedom, both from invasion by government under the guise of advancing the public interest
and from undermining by license with all its dangers.
The words of Madame Roland still echo across the
years, "O Liberty! how many crimes are committed in
thy name!"

The fundamental liberties of the individual are those
defined in our own national Bill of Rights. They are
freedom of religion, freedom of speech and of the press,
freedom of assembly, freedom to petition the government for a redress of grievances, and those other forms
of freedom which are defined in the first ten amend-
ments to the Federal Constitution. When that Constitution was under consideration, the opinion was expressed by many that the primary principles of civil
liberty might well be taken for granted and need not

be written into the new Constitution. The years which have followed afford abundant proof of the wisdom of those Founding Fathers who would take nothing of this kind for granted, but who insisted that a definition of the fundamental rights of the citizen be formally incorporated in the Constitution. Had this not been done, the history of the American people would have been very different from that which it now is. We have this clear-cut, fortunate and philosophically sound definition of our Liberty, and it is our highest duty to see to it that that Liberty be preserved and protected and not weakened, undermined or lost by careless indifference to attacks upon it, often well disguised and highly mischievous, from within. This means everything, not only to the people of the United States, but to the whole world of tomorrow.

Fundamentally, Equality means the equality of all in respect to civil, economic and political rights and equality before the law. It does not mean, and could not possibly mean, equality of individual ability, of individual capacity for achievement or in value of individual service to one's fellow men. Considerations of physical strength and health, of mental inheritance and equipment, and of environment, from all of which difference of opportunity arises, make such equality wholly impossible. No two individuals are ever exactly alike, and unless they were exactly alike, they could not possibly be equal in this mechanical sense. We see something which approaches mechanical equality among those confined in prison or those compelled to work either with hands or with brain under conditions rigorously imposed by a dominant power. Among a people which enjoys

Liberty, Equality quickly reveals itself by the rise to positions and opportunities of steadily increasing importance of those men and women who exhibit exceptional ability and capacity for achievement. In the industrial history of the American people there are illustrations without number of the capacity of the individual, given his opportunity, to rise to positions of high administrative power and responsibility solely by use of that equality of opportunity which our free institutions offer to him. Of those who are at the present time the chief administrative officers of twelve of our greatest railway systems, five began their service as clerks, two as office-boys, and one each as fireman and engineman, as track-laborer, as stenographer, as telegraph operator and as rod-man. This record tells its own story of the opportunity which is open to excellence. Many other similar instances could be found by an examination of our industrial and commercial organizations.

All those schemes of social, economic and political organization which would mechanically impose equality of service, of reward and of opportunity upon all, would invent a kind of Equality wholly out of consonance with Liberty. If that sort of Equality is to come first, then there will be no Liberty. The right to work, to earn and to save, and to use one's savings to increase production and to meet human needs, is fundamental to democracy. This right cannot be limited by any doctrine of permanent social and economic classes which are engaged in perpetual struggle for gain at each other's expense. Nor can it be limited by enforced membership in any group or organization—religious, political, social, economic, or industrial. Any such enforced limitation is not only undemocratic but it is anti-democratic. It is only Equality based upon Liberty, and which is Liberty's companion, that is real and which can carry civilization forward, generation after generation, through the efforts and the leadership of the most competent.

It is many years since I first had occasion to point out in a public address that a chief business of democracy is to produce its own aristocracy. That is the way in which democracy discovers those who are most competent to render it important and responsible service. It does this through the establishment of equality of opportunity in the field of Liberty. This democratic aristocracy will not be one based upon birth or inheritance. It will not be one based upon wealth or artificial advantage or upon that type of advantage which is known as privilege, but it will be one based only upon ability and capacity for achievement. That democracy will be most secure and most likely to last which can and does produce this aristocracy of its own and is guided by it.

Today the democracies, including our own, are subject to grave and in many ways deserved criticism because of the fact that they so often allow differences of opinion on minor matters and the passion for long-continued debate to postpone action at a time when their own prosperity, and indeed their own safety, depend upon their acceptance and support of a sound public policy adjusted to the needs of the moment. It is this characteristic, so often revealed in the recent history of the British, the French and the American democracies, which has led to the taunts, the cynicism and the sneers directed at them by the world's present-day despots and their groups of blindly devoted followers.

It is for a democracy quickly to make it plain that it can be and is an efficient form of government, and that neither Liberty nor Equality need be or will be weakened or sacrificed in order to attain efficiency of the highest order. We Americans can learn much from a study of the world's history during the past thirty years, as well as from a study of the problems which faced Abraham Lincoln and of those which face the President of the United States today. Quick and wise efficiency is the secret of their fortunate solution. One of Woodrow Wilson's wisest remarks was that "the highest and best form of efficiency is the spontaneous co-operation of a free people."

Given Liberty and Equality, there remains Fraternity. That is a state of mind and of conduct which is the outgrowth of Liberty and Equality working successfully together to guide an orderly, a progressive and a liberal society. Fraternity reveals itself in those hundred and one acts of kindly thoughtfulness and care which are in so large a degree characteristic of present-day America. It is the spirit of Fraternity which leads to great benefactions, made in the public interest by those who by reason of ability or good fortune have honestly acquired large wealth. Those who are really moved and guided by the fraternal spirit do not keep these vast fortunes for the members of their immediate families, but they bestow them in ·the public interest upon those institutions and undertakings which represent and reflect the fraternal spirit at its best. These are colleges and universities. They are hospitals and art museums. They are undertakings in the field of music and the fine arts. They are institutions to pro-

mote scientific discovery and application of new knowledge to the wants and needs of man. They are institutions for the care and guidance of the dependent and
of those who by reason of personal deficiency or disease
are unable to care for themselves. Were there no fraternal spirit, all such helpless individuals would be told
to care for themselves, and if they could not do so, to
pass out of existence and let nature take its course. That
is the barbaric but not the civilized method of dealing
with one's fellow men.

What is called Capital is civilization's greatest
achievement. Capital is what has been gained by work.
It is earnings and savings used to increase future production and to co-operate with others in multiplying that
production. The mother of Karl Marx was a very wise
woman, for she wrote: "If Karl had made a lot of Capital instead of writing a lot about Capital, it would have
been much better."[4] If one will read the story of the
life of Andrew Carnegie and of John D. Rockefeller
and see how, as unprecedented success attended their
life work, they had in mind from the very beginning the
service of their fellow men through the use of the fortunes, however large, which they might acquire, he will
see the working at its best of what is contemptuously
called the capitalistic system. Both Liberty and Equality would be far less efficient and far less deserving of
enthusiastic and devoted support were they not accompanied by Fraternity. It is Fraternity which learns the
lessons that Liberty and Equality have to teach and that
characterizes a social order made up of civilized human

[4]Beer, M., *The Life and Writings of Karl Marx.* (New York:
International Publishers (no date).) P. 31.

beings who will not willingly let their fellow men suffer or be in want.

Where, then, could we find for the guidance of tomorrow a motto more abundant in promise and more sound in principle than Liberty Equality Fraternity? To think that after receiving for a century and a half the approval and the applause of civilized men, this noble motto is now attacked and even ridiculed, is the best possible evidence of the backward character of the worldwide revolution which is under way and which has for the time being conquered France. If men were really civilized and if their word, formally and authoritatively given, could be depended upon, this backward revolution might have been much more speedily met and checked. It is only thirteen years since the governments of almost every nation in the world united with their fellow governments to renounce war as an instrument of national policy and to proceed to the settlement of international differences and disputes in a spirit of peaceful discussion and judicial determination. The ink was hardly dry upon this great treaty known as the Pact of Paris when some of the governments which had signed it began to prepare for war more vigorously than ever before in history. Their men of science were set to the invention and perfection of new instruments for military use. The children in their schools were disciplined and trained not to enjoy and to understand Liberty, but to do as they were told, to obey without question and to submit to the emotional guidance of formulas and phrases, every one of which meant war and preparation for war. It was those nations which accepted the Pact of Paris in the spirit in which they signed it that did not engage in these preparations and that, therefore, were the first subject of attack when the new despots undertook to take over the rule of the world for the establishment of their New Order. The democracies lagged in military preparation, and they lagged because their peoples believed what their governments had said and were innocent enough to take it for granted that all other signatory powers were honest and faith-keeping. Such is the explanation of much which is now going on all about us, of the undermining of national spirit and national unity of purpose by every sort and kind of public enemy, and which has led to the pathetic downfall of France and the literally appalling attack upon Great Britain and its people. This is neither the time nor the place to attempt a forecast of what the immediate future has in store. If, by any fortunate chance, the chief enemies of Liberty, Equality and Fraternity, which are now carrying on a stupendous military contest between themselves, should wreck and ruin each other, the door would be open to a new era of progress, provided the democracies have the insight, the courage and the intellectual capacity to take the lead in organizing a truly new world on those principles of Liberty, Equality and Fraternity which must rule if prosperity and peace are to return and to endure. The federal principle has now established itself in so many forms and over so many different areas that there can be no question but that it will afford the key to the solution of the chief political problems which world organization has to offer. That economic nationalism which has had so much to do with promoting world confusion, world competition and world war, must give way to that international trade system which great seers like Adam Smith and Richard Cobden, John Bright and Gladstone long ago saw to be as necessary as it is sound. There is no more reason why every independent sovereign nation should supply all of the physical wants of its own people from territory under its own flag than there is that it should supply all of their intellectual wants and needs from men of science, men of letters and intellectual leaders who speak that language and who owe that allegiance. Ideas go about the world with instant speed and without obstruction. Why should not men's economic needs be satisfied in like fashion? All that is required to answer this question is high intelligence, insight, courage and adherence to the motto, Liberty Equality Fraternity.

For the time being, the people of France have been compelled, officially at least, to turn their back upon those noble words. They have been flatly told that their system of free, democratic government has broken down and that there is no way by which it can be re-established. Government by decree, through the agency of definite and fixed economic or social groups or classes, is hailed as the substitute for democracy and its hopeful successor. What is called "this reformation" is to be brought about by selection of the élite from all rungs of the social ladder. This selection, however, is not to be made through Equality of opportunity for all, but by the definite act of a higher and controlling power. In other words, "by decree" is to take the place of democratic legislation. Surely, as great a people as the French will not permit so reactionary a condition as this to remain forever. The intellectual history of the French people is so superb that their intellectual life cannot die.

It may be for the time being in a state of coma or it may be held in chains, but it will return to its self-control, to its freedom and then, sobered and disciplined by the experiences of this generation, it will write those words Liberty Equality Fraternity upon hundreds of walls, this time to remain for ages to come.

The opportunity of world leadership, now offered to the American people, is so unprecedented that our responsibility is too great to be measured in ordinary words. When world leadership was with Greece and then with Rome, civilization, however magnificent in its intellectual manifestations, was so simple and so undeveloped in the economic and industrial fields that what the Greeks and Romans were able to accomplish was quickly made plain and written into history. Conditions today are not only different, but wholly new. This twentieth-century world of nearly one hundred separate national units has cherished the hope and the belief that each national unit, whether large or small, might be made secure and protected in its national independence by international co-operation, international law and the judicial settlement of international disputes. The American people have been committed to these principles from the very beginning of their history. They have cherished them, they have hailed them, and time and time again they have given vigorous and emphatic illustration of their faith in them. Unless the small national group can be protected by its fellow national units, there can be neither Liberty nor Equality nor Fraternity in the national and international life of the world. It is idle to use these words as applicable only to individual life and thought and conduct. They must also be applicable to national policy and to international life and thought and conduct. If the American people can lead the thought of the world to turn its back upon any system of social, economic or political organization which rests upon fixed and definite classes or groups with a resulting spirit of class consciousness, then indeed will the door be open to the progress of a truly liberal philosophy of life and of government. The call of today and tomorrow is to the people of the United States. Will they hear that call? And will they answer it in the spirit of their great forefathers—of Washington and of Franklin, of Hamilton and of Jefferson, of Madison and of Marshall, of Webster and of Lincoln? If they will, the future peace and prosperity of this now torn and broken world will be as secure as human thought and human power can make it.

II

IS THOMAS JEFFERSON THE FORGOTTEN MAN?

An address delivered
at the Parrish Memorial Art Museum
Southampton, Long Island
September 1, 1935

IS THOMAS JEFFERSON THE
FORGOTTEN MAN?

Men are making a mess of the business of government almost everywhere. They have pretty clearly
demonstrated their capacity to do better anything and
everything within the reach of their powers than to care
in organized fashion and under legal forms for those
common interests and ideals which free men have shown
themselves ready and willing to commit to Government. It is probable that in Sweden, in the Netherlands
and in Great Britain governmental action and policy
conform more fully to instructed and disinterested public opinion than elsewhere in the world, but even in
those countries, particularly in Great Britain, Government has many and vigorous critics. The fact of the
matter is that civilization, with the grouping of human
beings together in organized society, depends for its
advance in terms of Liberty upon the capacity and will-
ingness of individual human beings to bear their re-
spective parts not primarily in a spirit of gain-seeking
but in a spirit of service, leaving therefore to Government only the most elementary duties and functions. In
so far as there is failure to reach this level of excellence,
and in so far as the profit motive fails in subordination
to the spirit of service, there is constant turning to Government for relief from real or fancied abuses. If the

endeavor to subordinate the spirit of gain-seeking to the spirit of service shall prove to be permanently beyond the reach of human beings, then there will be and must be a continual drift through Government toward some form of despotism or compulsion, in the hope of thereby achieving ends that seem otherwise unattainable. This is precisely the point which the world has reached in this year of grace 1935.

There are some fundamental principles taught by reason and upheld by experience which must not be forgotten. When Wallace and Darwin expounded the theory of organic evolution, they pointed to a fact which is basic in the constitution and development of human society. That fact is the survival of those who are best fitted and adapted to their environment. This means that success will take place side by side with failure, that excellence will exhibit itself side by side with incompetence and that high-minded, constructive service will be found side by side with mean-spirited envy, hatred and malice. It takes all sorts of human beings to make this world. Not only is it a fact that individuals are not and cannot be equal in respect to physical force or technical skill or intellectual power or moral excellence, but that all progress would come to an end if they were. If there be no higher end at which to aim than this equality, then the stagnation of death will displace the activity of life. These differences between individuals which have been and are the moving cause of all progress in the history of civilization, must be reckoned with as permanent forces, unless through their extermination we propose to bring civilization to an end. This is why all forms of collectivism are of necessity reactionary and can, in the end, bring only unhappiness, suffering and disaster to those masses which they are supposed to be able to aid. The real problem here is not to suppress or to limit individual ability or individual activity, or to prevent that man who can do better work than his fellows with his hands or with his head from enjoying the fruit of his labors and of whatever he may be able to save from his earnings after having met his comfortable living costs. The task before the world is not the suppression, much less the elimination, of individual excellence and its adaptation to environment, but rather the control and shaping of environment so as to bring reasonable adaptation to it within the reach of the largest possible number of individual human beings. Almost all the radical movements and undertakings of the moment aim at the suppression of individual excellence and are therefore in flat contradiction with Liberalism in any of its forms. They are not only reactionary but gravely damaging to the highest and largest interests of society as a whole. In some form, the doctrine of collective despotism has been taught from time to time since civilization began but it has never made any considerable headway until the present generation.

Probably at no time in history have fundamental principles of political organization and administration been examined and debated with larger insight and understanding than when the government of the United States was in the making. Mr. Gladstone was certainly justified in his famous panegyric upon the work of the Constitutional Convention of 1787, the membership of which was described by Thomas Jefferson as an assemblage of demigods. For reasons which it is not difficult to understand, it has been customary to set Alexander Hamilton and Thomas Jefferson in sharp opposition, the one to the other, as political philosophers intimately concerned with the shaping of American political thought and with the organization and functions of the federal system of government which was so fortunately adopted. A wiser view, however, and one which is amply justified by the happenings of the past century and a half, is that which regards the teachings of Hamilton and of Jefferson as not so much in opposition to each other as complementary to each other. Hamilton, as his great papers amply record, was profoundly concerned with the adequacy of the powers of the federal government and with its ability and capacity to establish financial and economic policies that would be in the largest public interest. Thomas Jefferson, on the other hand, was looking chiefly at the relation of Government to the individual and his freedom, and he never ceased insisting upon the truth that in a land of free men, Government is the servant of the citizen and that the citizen is not the servant of Government. Alexander Hamilton was quickly successful in establishing his policies and ideals, and through the judicial interpretation of the Constitution by Chief Justice Marshall these became the accepted foundation upon which the national life rests. Oddly enough, however, despite Jefferson's great authority and the long-continuing power of the political party which he called into being, it is his principles and teachings which at this very moment are most vigorously attacked and contradicted. It is a queer happening in the history of American politics that the chief instrumentality for contradicting Thomas Jefferson should be the present-day leaders of the political party of which he was the inspiration. For two generations that party in the platforms adopted by its quadrennial national conventions found some way in which to acclaim Jefferson and to pay tribute to his name and fame. In fact, his name is mentioned specifically in the platforms adopted by the National Democrat Party in 1840, in 1892, in 1896, in 1900, in 1904, in 1908, in 1912, in 1924 and in 1928. On the other hand, the opposition party, the Republican, which has continued in our public life the spirit and the ideals of Hamilton and which has uniformly treated the name of Thomas Jefferson with more or less unconcern, is now vigorously preaching his doctrines and calling upon men to return to their defense and re-establishment. Can it be that Thomas Jefferson is the forgotten man? Has that great dominant personality, touching life at so many points and inspiring men and policies of such various kinds, who passed from earth on July 4, 1826, already been forgotten? Every believer in governmental regimentation of business, of agriculture or of industry contradicts Thomas Jefferson. Every Communist, every Nazi, every Fascist and every American sympathizer with any of these forms of government and social organization contradicts Thomas Jefferson. May it not be worth while briefly to inquire how far Thomas Jefferson was wrong and whether these new and disturbing forms of compulsion now urged as substitutes for Liberty are to be accepted as sounder teachings than those of Jefferson?

One suspects that it is the wicked profit motive which is once more at work and that what these advocates of compulsion have really in mind is not an advancing and improved civilization, with larger measure of satisfaction and happiness for each and all, so much as a personal share in the results of the labors and savings of other men. In other words, the moving force is not moral but economic. It is not service to mankind but gain-seeking for the individual. At this point we begin to see that all Share-the-Wealth programs are misnamed. They really should be called Steal-the-Wealth programs. It is not their intention to provide new and larger opportunities for fruitful labor, whether by hand or by brain, but rather to take by force some part of those savings which the work and the thrift of others have enabled them to build up. One of John Marshall's famous phrases was that the power to tax involves the power to destroy. He might have gone farther and said that the power to tax is the power to effect revolution and to overturn any established form of free government. As a matter of fact, those statesmen who insisted that a Bill of Rights should be included in, or attached to, the Constitution of the United States at the time that the federal government was set up, were not only sound in their thinking but they were prophets as well. It is this Bill of Rights which is fundamental to the American form of government, and its principles, although not written in words, are also basic in the government of Great Britain. The purpose of the Bill of Rights was to protect the individual against the worst, the most cruel and the most selfish of all despotisms, which is that of the majority. The doctrine that the majority must rule is merely a convenient way of saying that up to the present time no better way has been found of testing the public opinion of a community than by asking its members to vote on some specific proposal or undertaking. But this rule of the majority is definitely restricted, both in Great Britain and still more specifically in the United States, by those fundamental principles of civic, economic and political liberty which are set forth in the Bill of Rights.

It is with these facts in mind that all schemes and plans of taxation are to be examined and tested. If a tax be fairly and equitably levied upon individuals and undertakings in accordance with their ability to pay and with the lowest possible exemption, to the end that every one who votes for those who are to spend public money shall be tax-conscious and therefore quick to resent and to rebuke governmental extravagance, we are on sound and wholly defensible ground. When, however, the power to tax is used for the purpose of punishing individuals or groups, or for the purpose of effecting, whether consciously or unconsciously, economic, social or political revolution, then every principle which the American people hold most dear is under attack and in danger of fatal damage or overthrow. "Unnecessary taxation is unjust taxation," says the Democrat National platform of 1884, written chiefly by no less a man than Abram S. Hewitt. It cannot be too insistently repeated that the tyranny and compulsion of a majority, usually temporary, exercised through the power of taxation, without reference to the Bill of Rights or to moral principle, is the most dangerous enemy which Liberty has to face. It is more insidious than Communism, and its dangers are less likely to be quickly recognized than those which are characteristic of Nazism or of Fascism. These facts are an added argument for the

Bill of Rights and for defending the individual, through his protection by the judicial power as established in the Constitution, from invasion and tyranny by Government. All this used to be considered fundamental American doctrine and while it often required interpretation, it rarely excited debate. We have now, however, come face to face with the rising wave of compulsion which has already in a great part of the world completely overwhelmed and swamped the growing Liberalism of the past three hundred years and which is in our own country moving vigorously in many different ways toward the same end. If the taxing power be habitually used, not to support through a balanced budget an economical and wisely administered government which is minding its own proper business, but rather to discriminate against and to punish individuals, undertakings and groups, then, without having amended our Constitution in any way, we shall have well begun to undermine its foundations.

What is the reason and the excuse for all this? In Russia, it is the clever seizing of power by a group of economic doctrinaires who found the ground prepared for them by centuries of Czarist despotism over a vast population, largely ignorant, untutored and out of touch with the world. In Italy, Fascism made its appeal when a forceful and dominant personality voiced its doctrines and offered active organization to a people which had become discouraged and, politically speaking, restless and discontented. In Germany, the conditions are distinctly psychopathic. The cruel mistakes which were made when the Treaty of Versailles was dictated and not negotiated, when the foolish paragraph as to the sole war guilt of the Germans was insisted upon, when every sort and kind of discrimination was made against a proud, if defeated, people who had for two full centuries made powerful and permanent contribution to the world's philosophy, the world's literature, the world's science and the world's art, well prepared the way for what has been happening in Germany. When the former Allies insisted upon their domineering attitude even after the Pact of Locarno had been signed and after Germany had joined the League of Nations, and when the forward-facing policies of Stresemann and Briand were blocked at every turn by reactionary and ultra-nationalistic forces, the path was certainly paved for the success of any leader with a voice and a personality which would appeal to a people's wounded pride and injured feelings. This is precisely what happened with the advent of Hitler. The real Germany, the true Germany, the historic Germany, is for the moment in eclipse, and we have a nation-wide psychopathic phenomenon with millions listening to preposterous, unhistoric and unscientific doctrines and teachings as to race, as to religion and as to a nation's place in the world. Time and time alone can cure such a condition as this. But the blame must not be put wholly upon the German people by any means. The rest of the world must take its full share of the blame for having made these present conditions possible and having brought them about.

When we turn to the United States and reflect upon the history of the past quarter-century, it becomes obvious that it has not been Liberty but the abuses of Liberty, it has not been the Bill of Rights but the shocking acts of groups and individuals under the protection of the Bill of Rights, which have so affronted and outraged millions of the American people that for the moment their eyes seem closed to the fundamental principles upon which their government and social order rest and upon which these must rest if they are to continue. So violent and so dishonest were many manifestations of the profit motive, so unjust, so immoral and so far-reaching were many of its deeds, that men became first suspicious, then angry, then so hopeless that they began to open their hearts and minds to political acts and policies which under ordinary circumstances would have been most repugnant to them. Once again we see here the perpetual conflict between economics and morals, between the profit motive and the spirit of service. Given the field of Liberty occupied and developed by the profit motive, with the spirit of service in the background or wholly forgotten, and the door is quickly opened for that revolution, whether silent or forcible, by which compulsion will enter to take Liberty's place.

The history of Government both in Great Britain and in the United States makes it pretty plain that free government functions best—and perhaps can only function at all—under the two-party system. The two essential parties correspond to two clearly marked types of human mind and human feeling. The one wishes to go ahead and make changes; the other wishes to keep things substantially as they are and to combat changes when proposed. Therefore the one party is Liberal or Progressive and the other is Conservative. These two parties and the two types of mind which they represent fit themselves to the framework of almost any form of free government. Each party is very critical of the other and it gains power when its criticisms are successful in convincing public opinion. The two-party system prevailed in the United States from a few years after the establishment of the federal government until the present generation. It has now disappeared in all but name and therefore the American people are now without one of the most powerful instruments of political effectiveness. What was the Republican Party went on the rocks in 1912 and while there are still many millions of Republicans throughout the country, they are without any common body of political principle and without any definite political program. The historic Democrat Party was practically destroyed by Bryan and has never been rehabilitated and reunited. We must not be misled by appearances; there are parties but only in name. Many of those who call themselves Republicans and many of those who call themselves Democrats are in flat contradiction as to many fundamental principles and policies with others who claim the same party name. This illogical and, indeed, ludicrous situation has contributed mightily to bring our government to its present unhappy pass. We can no longer trust the promises and pledges of a political platform, because when elected, those who bear the party name may, and often do, treat that platform with entire unconcern and sometimes with flat contradiction. What then are the American people voting for and how is public opinion to make itself effectively felt in official public action? Just now these are pressing practical problems in the United States. If and when men use party names and party traditions to secure popular support and then when elected to office throw their influence and their votes in favor of measures which flatly contradict the principles and traditions of that party whose name they profess to bear, how are we to carry on free government? If this sort of thing continues, the American people will find themselves face to face with chaos instead of with orderly government. One active, well-organized, self-seeking minority after another will control public policy for its own selfish purposes, no matter at what cost of fundamental principle or of the general welfare.

Surely it is a sad commentary upon the conditions which now confront us that, to speak bluntly, so many thousands of the American people have shown clearly that they are for sale. We have been familiar for generations with the fact that a candidate for public office could best endear himself to his constituency by securing appropriations of public money to be spent on public projects within the state or district from which he had been elected to office. When Thomas B. Reed of Maine was speaker of the House of Representatives some forty years ago, he took occasion to denounce with the utmost vigor the activities of those Congressmen who, under pressure from their several districts, labored to secure the expenditure of public monies therein for purposes which were, in no proper sense of the word, necessary. Unhappily, there are no Thomas B. Reeds now visible above the office-holding horizon, and quite another state of mind is daily revealing itself. For the old-fashioned, upstanding, independent Americanism, there is now substituted in words of pathetic surrender "Let Government do it." Tens of thousands of men and women who are receiving government relief are reported to resist going to work in honorable employment because they prefer the certainty and security of the government payment. This is shocking indeed, and it reveals a complete undermining of the American character by the profit motive. If there be any one end to which we must address ourselves more than another, it is the rehabilitation of the American independence of mind, of body and of estate.

As matters now stand, we are permitting, often without realizing it, the steady transfer to the field of Government of activities which belong in the field of Liberty. This means not only a complete change of national character and institutions but also a vast lowering of effectiveness in a host of agencies for the public service; for it is quite certain that whatever Government undertakes to do in the field of agriculture, of industry, of commerce or of philanthropy, it will do far less well than individual citizens co-operating together to work in the field of Liberty under the inspiration of the motive of service. It is by subtly drifting policies of this kind that our social, economic and political life can be swept from its moorings and that we may be carried over into a form of collectivism that will leave Communism with all its horrors, its sufferings and its fatal losses, only a short distance away. There is small use in punishing and deporting Communists if we permit the steady application of Communist principles in our national life.

Unhappily, the fact is constantly overlooked that in our American life and social order the words Public on the one hand and Official or Government on the other are by no means interchangeable. As a matter of fact, by far the major portion of our public service is rendered in the field of Liberty and not by Government at all. Over and above such outstanding illustrations as hospitals, asylums, colleges and universities upon which Government could not lay its hand without greatly reducing their usefulness, there are literally tens of thousands of public service undertakings, large and small, being carried on throughout the country with amazing effectiveness by individual and group effort. This service is none the less public because it is unofficial; indeed, it is more important and more effective just because it is unofficial. If Government, by abuse of the taxing power which is within its control, destroys the ability of hundreds of thousands of individual men and women to join in carrying forward these various types of public service, then Government is striking a treacherous blow at the public interest which can only be followed by a literally incalculable damage and loss. All these considerations enforce the conviction that Thomas Jefferson was right; that Government must be carefully restricted in its powers and functions; that it must be held closely to them; and that every attempt on the part of Government to invade the reserved field of Liberty, no matter on what pretense, must be stoutly and stubbornly resisted.

If it be said that conditions have changed since Jefferson's day and that we must now be prepared to face the complex social, economic and political problems of the twentieth century with open minds and without reference to what was said by Hamilton, by Jefferson or by any other of the Founding Fathers, the answer is Yes, that is true but with a very important qualification. Fundamental principles do not change, no matter what happens to the environment in which their application is sought or attempted. The multiplication table does not change, the rule of three does not change, the moral law does not change. What changes is the environment. Just so the sound principles which Jefferson taught have lost nothing of their soundness because of the altered conditions under which they are to be practically applied. If we are to maintain and enjoy Liberty, nothing is more certain than that we in the United States—leaving other peoples out of consideration for the moment—must see to it that the privileges and rights of Liberty are not abused by dominance of the profit-seeking motive, so that individuals and groups are oppressed, imposed upon or exploited. That all of these things have happened during the past generation is unfortunately true, but now the public is awake to the character and cause of these happenings and will see to it that they are not continued or repeated. The proper function of Government in matters of this kind is not to take control of the details of business or business organization in any of their forms, but rather to supervise, to criticize and to punish infractions of the rules of law and the principles of sound morals. Far from discouraging individuals and groups in their efforts to develop agriculture, industry and commerce and to multiply various forms of public service, Government should do everything in its power to remove obstacles to the successful carrying forward of these undertakings. Public opinion must see to it that the public service motive is in control and that the profit-seeking motive is subordinated to it. This will not be easy, human nature being constituted as it is, but it will be far easier to accomplish this end through efforts in the field of Liberty than to attempt to do so through the bureaucratic and legalistic action of Government. Any effort of the latter kind can only do more harm than good to the interest of the whole people. For example, the vengeful desire on the part of Government to place an inordinately high tax upon personal and corporate incomes and upon personal estates will shortly be seen to have a profoundly disturbing effect on the general welfare. On the surface, a policy of this kind simply strips individuals and families of especially large accumulations of wealth, but looked at more closely, it disturbs and disarranges the whole of the American social order. It must quickly bring about the dismissal from their welcome occupations at satisfactory compensation, not of tens of thousands, but of hundreds of thousands of men and women who are happily and satisfactorily employed. It must disarrange and cripple in a thousand unsuspected and unexpected ways the nation's industry and commerce; and when the end shall have been reached what will it amount to? Nothing but to satisfy the incredibly mean desire to punish those who are more fortunate than most of us. Where these great accumulations of wealth have come to pass by fraud, by exploitation or by lawlessness, let there be punishment to the limit. Nothing could be more false, however, than the assumption that because an individual or a group possesses a large accumulation of wealth this has been brought about by unjust or improper means. Such is not true in one case out of twenty. Any attempt to attack these citizens through a misuse of the taxing power will punish thrift and wisdom twenty times where it will punish wrongdoing once. This is a fact to be insistently drummed into the heads of those who, temporarily in important public office, use the power of that office with malice and bitterness to damage those who have been more fortunate or more thrifty than themselves.

One must wonder why it is that the possessors of honorably acquired great fortunes do not see the wisdom of giving or leaving by far the greater part of these fortunes to institutions and undertakings in the fields of Liberty which have the highest type of public service as their aim. One would think that the examples of Carnegie, of Harkness, of Rockefeller and a few others would have their effect and would lead others to satisfy and to gratify the public by devoting the major portion of their accumulations to the public service. Were this more commonly done, there would be far less criticism than is now the case of the possessors of these great fortunes, provided, of course, that they had come honestly and fairly by them.

Thomas Jefferson was fundamentally right in his political philosophy and it is high time that he was rescued, not by one political party but by all Americans, from being the Forgotten Man which he now so obviously is. It is wholly practicable, without in any way disturbing the foundations of our American government and social system, without farther amending the Constitution and without doing violence to the underlying principles of the finest and most progressive Liberalism, to offer solution for all of the new problems with which the changing social, economic and political environment has brought us face to face. To do this, however, we must first of all rid ourselves of the dogmatic and baseless Marxian assumptions and absurdities which are just now so much in evidence. There are no fixed and definite classes in the United States, and there is no proletariat here. One need only read the family history of those who have come to positions of high importance in business, in social or in political life to see what their origins were and how completely those origins were shared by millions of their fellow citizens. With us the door of opportunity is always open to ability, to skill, to capacity and to high character. He who labors with his hands today may be found laboring with his head tomorrow and directing and guiding the labor of others shortly thereafter. Not only have we no classes in the United States, but it is vitally important that we permit none to grow up among us. To prevent the appearance of fixed and definite classes in our social order, public opinion must be relied upon, since no other force can avail. In city and in country, in east and in west, in north and in south, we must all concern ourselves with the health of the people, with the housing of the people, with the conditions under which work, whether by hand or by brain, is carried on, as well as with fair and generous compensation for such work with definite assurance against the tragedy of unemployment, of illness or of dependent old age. All these things can and will be provided for within the field of Liberty, Government being called upon from time to time only for its cooperation, its supervision and its criticism. No political and social system in this twentieth century can rest upon a sound moral foundation which does not do these things and do them well. When the profit motive is found to be harassing those who work with hand or with brain, by too long hours of labor, by too small compensation, by the employment of children or in any other way, then public opinion must teach that profit motive its place and subordinate it to the larger, finer and more humane view, which is that given us by the spirit of service.

When anything goes wrong in the United States, the usual and very prompt reaction is to demand the passage of some new law. The result is that our statute books are literally clogged with thousands of useless and futile provisions of law which accomplish nothing and which in due time pass into what Grover Cleveland happily described as innocuous desuetude. Law is but one of several methods of social control, and it is astonishing how little it can accomplish, even in regard to such a crime as murder as to which it would seem easily dominant. Murder, for example, has been against the law ever since Moses came down from Mount Sinai, and yet there were more murders in the United States last year than ever before in our history. For century upon century murderers have been executed either by torture, by beheading, by hanging or by electrocution. Nevertheless, murders continue to multiply in every part of the world. What this means is that what law cannot do must be left for accomplishment to the often slow-moving force of public opinion with its organized agencies of education, the family, the school and the church. No nation can be made wise or public spirited or liberal-minded by law. Law can help mightily, but it is always and everywhere subordinate to public opinion and to those great intangible forces—emotional, intellectual, moral—which so constantly sweep over masses of men. It is these which we ourselves must learn to guide and to control. Then Government will be in its proper place and Thomas Jefferson will have won another victory.

III

THE CLOSE OF AN EPOCH

An address delivered at the Annual Meeting
of the Pilgrims of the United States, New York
January 22, 1936

THE CLOSE OF AN EPOCH

We are met in the shadow of a great sorrow. Our brother Pilgrims of Great Britain, their millions of fellow citizens and the tens of millions living on every continent and under every clime who owe allegiance to some member of the British Commonwealth of Nations, are stricken with sadness and a deep sense of loss by the death of their Monarch. That is no ordinary happening. That we in America appreciate that fact is amply demonstrated by the widespread public interest in everything which relates to the life of the King and to his passing, and by the quite exceptional emphasis laid upon it all by our press.

The sympathy of the American people and their interest have been aroused anew because of their understanding of the significance of this sorrow and the sympathy which they feel for the British people.

It is difficult for us fully to appreciate the position of their Monarch in the life and work of the British people. It is quite different from that of those former-time emperors and kings who were personal rulers and who themselves exercised directly the highest functions of government. The happenings of the past two hundred and fifty years have brought into existence in Great Britain a new type of government and one peculiarly adapted to the traditions and habits of the English people. That new form of government is the democratic monarchy. This monarchy, while hereditary, rests upon the will of the people, and has done so for nearly two hundred and fifty years. It has taken the major portion of that time, however, for the monarch to develop that personal relationship to public life and to government which now exists in so satisfactory a form.

We who live in a democratic republic find it difficult sometimes to trace analogies between the organization and the operation of our democratic republic and those of a democratic monarchy. But the analogy is close enough. In our democratic republic based upon a written constitution, definite in form and in terms, we have set up a threefold organization of government. We have given to each definite duties and responsibilities. As is sometimes forgotten, each of the three directly represents the people. The President is their choice as chief executive. The national legislature is their choice to give voice to the convictions, the ideas, the tendencies, the policies of the moment. The United States Supreme Court is their voice to give calm and reasoned expression to their fundamental and everlasting principles and ideals. They have provided in their government, these American people, for this form of dealing with public policy and public business.

The democratic monarchy is more analogous than sometimes is obvious, and yet, it has very marked differences. Inasmuch as the Constitution of Great Britain is not fixed and definite, but is a matter of tradition and of habit, its interpretation is not by judicial voice but by legislative act. When, as in the Parliament Act of 1911 or as in the Statute of Westminster of 1931, a grave step is taken in changing the organization of the British Government, what they are really doing is amending their constitution thereby. That is why they do not have judicial interpretation of their Constitution, because not being written, not being definite, it can and must be dealt with as habit and necessity may require, by the action of the legislative branch of their government.

And moreover, instead of separating, as we have done, the executive and the legislative branches of the government, they have subordinated their executive to the legislative, except when the executive is powerful enough to make the legislative carry out its will. Therefore it is that the administrative side of the British Government, the ministry, must command a parliamentary majority. When the parliamentary majority fails, the administration falls or is changed.

What, then, is left for the Monarch? The Monarch becomes the fortunate symbol of the nation's unity, of the nation's faith and of the nation's ideals. He is above, out of and beyond current political and partisan discussions, no matter what his personal feelings or preferences may be. He stands, therefore, to represent the people as a whole in their political and in their non-political life and organization. Therefore, if he has their confidence as King George V had in so high degree, he strengthens every part of the British Commonwealth of Nations through the force of his personality.

It would be a great mistake to suppose that the King has no influence upon what happens in public life. Let one read the Letters of Queen Victoria, or more recently, the Memoirs of Sir Almeric Fitzroy, who was for twenty-five years Clerk of the Privy Council, and there you will find recorded time and time again how the monarch by his tact, by his skill, by his kindliness, has helped to bridge over a difficulty, has helped to formulate a policy, has helped to carry out some forward step in the life of the British people as he cannot do publicly or with authority. That is the field in which personality matters, and the monarch who can do that for a people as liberal, as forward-facing and as highly intelligent as the British and who can make his appeal, as George V did, to the entire British Commonwealth of Nations, must be a very remarkable human being.

It is but a few months since the whole world was listening to the public celebration of the twenty-fifth anniversary of the Monarch's succession. We remember with satisfaction and with pride how from every part of the world, not only the British Commonwealth of Nations, but from Europe, Asia, Africa and the Americas, there came expressions of confidence and satisfaction and praise. That is a great achievement, and King George V in passing away so soon after that world-wide celebration gives new significance to its meaning and to its importance.

How striking it is that the King should pass away almost at the same moment as that poet who more than any other in the history of the English language has sounded every note and touched every string of the imperial life and the imperial spirit. If in the life of our literature there was any voice to play the part, a similar part, to that which the King himself played in the public and social life of the Empire, it was Rudyard Kipling. That extraordinary person, dying at seventy, had written almost every one of his great verses and pieces of prose more than thirty-five years ago. His genius ripened in youth and early manhood. Then it was with the vigor of youth and the prescience of a sound philosophy of life, he looked out over the world and saw the significance of his many-sided people and celebrated it in verse, much of which is immortal. The man who could write "On the Road to Mandalay," the "Hymn Before Actim," "Fuzzy-Wuzzy," "The Long Trail," "Gunga Din," and that stately and superb "Recessional," was a great poet of the British Empire.

Surely, my fellow Pilgrims, it closes an epoch when this noble Monarch who had lived successfully through so many world-troubled years, and this man of letters who had seen the picture of those years and painted it —surely, it is an inspiration for us to think of them and what they meant as they lay down their lives upon the altar of immortality. They represent, the King in his way, Rudyard Kipling in his way, that great and splendid tradition which is ours. They stood in their acts and in their words for our inheritance on which we so like to dwell. How can we better phrase our reflection upon them than in these splendid words of Kipling himself?

> Our Fathers in a wondrous age
> Ere yet the Earth was small,
> Ensured to us a heritage,
> And doubted not at all
> That we, the children of their heart,
> Which then did beat so high,
> In later time should play like part
> For our posterity.

IV

THE BACKGROUND OF THE LABOR
PROBLEM

An address delivered at the Parrish Memorial Art Museum
Southampton, Long Island, September 5, 1937

THE BACKGROUND OF THE LABOR PROBLEM

Speaking in this place one year ago, I named the regulation of trade disputes as one of the six major problems confronting our people and our government at the present time. It was then pointed out that those of us who work, whether with our hands or with our brains, constitute an overwhelming proportion of the population of any modern state and that therefore the interests of those who work, taken in the larger sense, are identical with the interests of the public as a whole. It was pointed out that disputes between those who work and those for whom they work are steadily increasing in number and in violence, and that these disputes are now commonly accompanied by strikes, which are a form of war. Attention was called to some of the steps which had recently been taken, particularly in Great Britain, to regulate and to govern these trade disputes and to prevent them from becoming a damage and a danger to the interests of the general public.

During the year which has passed, this matter has taken on new and menacing importance. It is high time that American public opinion rose to the height of its responsibility for bringing into existence such policies as will protect the interests of the public and the principles of our government from the devastating effects of that form of economic war which has come to be the very ordinary and usual accompaniment of trade disputes. This matter cannot be permitted to drift indefinitely without very grave consequences. It is of highest importance that these problems be not looked upon solely in their superficial aspect or from the viewpoint of those immediately concerned and the pressure groups which they organize, but that the forces and aims which underlie and shape them be brought to light and interpreted.

From the dawn of history, the human race has been engaged in one sort of struggle after another. At the beginning, individuals struggled with their environment in order to protect themselves against wild animals and to secure the wherewithal to maintain existence. As time went on and civilization took definite form and developed various social, economic and political institutions, however simple, this struggle became one of group against group and eventually of nation against nation. Within a given nation, men found themselves, either by temperament, by ambition or by necessity, thrown into more or less close and continuing contact with others who were pursuing the same activities as themselves. These groups have been described by historians as social classes. There was a time when the priestly class was eager to establish its control and superiority over both those who were engaged in military activities and those who were developing some form of industry. Later on, the landholders came to be a group by themselves, and for long generations the feudal system was the result. With the rise of modern industries and the application to human needs of the astounding scientific discoveries of the past century and a half, there came a new division between those who work for wages and salaries and those who are, or who represent, the owners of capital by means of which industries are carried on.

It is important to realize that these group struggles and group ambitions are natural, not artificial, and that they are the outgrowth in large part of difference in human capacity and intelligence, as well as of difference in social, economic and political opportunity and environment. It must be realized that with the advent of democracy it was no longer necessary or even possible for these groups or classes to be permanent and fixed in their membership, even if such had been the case in earlier times. It is of the essence of democracy that there be equality of opportunity for all men and that each and all be invited and tempted to exert themselves to the utmost in order that the society of which they are a part may have the fullest benefit of their abilities and their knowledge, as well as in order that they themselves may pass easily and quickly from one group or class to another according as circumstances invite and permit. In a democracy there is and can be no place for fixed and definite social, economic or political classes. Other and non-democratic forms of government may permit or require these, but democracy cannot do so without turning its back upon its fundamental principles. Therefore it is that persistent care must be taken to prevent these natural and normal struggles between individuals and groups from developing into a class struggle or class war between groups whose membership is fixed and definitely settled beyond hope of change.

The doctrine that all history is to be interpreted in terms of a class war between those who possess and those who do not, however popular it seemed at one time, is crude, unhistorical and untrue as a matter of fact. The economic interpretation of history is important but subordinate, as Professor Seligman conclusively proved a generation ago.[1] There can be no question, however, that the economic aspect of history has taken on greatly increased significance during the past century because of the world-wide rise on a huge scale of the industrial system with which we are now familiar. In any large sense, neither the national market nor the world market existed prior to the seventeenth century. Down to that time, industry and trade were dominated by the needs and possibilities of a market that was strictly local. Then, with world-wide exploration and settlement came new conditions which paved the way, first for the displacement of the local market by the national market, and then for the addition of the theretofore unknown world market. It is the national market and the world market which are at this moment engaged in a struggle for dominance, the outcome of which will determine the history of our civilization for generations to come. Economic nationalism is today engaged in the perfectly futile endeavor to make the national market independent of the world market, a policy which can have but one end, and that is overwhelming disaster to the nations themselves which undertake to pursue it.

Karl Marx, who with all his limitations and shortcomings was the possessor of an acute intellect, said

[1]Seligman, Edwin R. A., *The Economic Interpretation of History* (New York: Columbia University Press, 1902).

nearly a century ago that "The relation of industry and of the world of wealth in general to the political world is the chief problem of modern times."[2] This is profoundly true, but it must not be forgotten that in approaching the industrial problem of today we are face to face with tendencies and movements which have existed since civilization began, with an economic condition in which the whole world is a possible market for the product of any industry, and in which industry itself has developed in so remarkable a degree that it has made its interests and its problems of outstanding importance, not only in the economic but in the political life of the present-day world.

There are some popular, almost ruling, misconceptions which should be cleared away. Of these the chief is that there is a social and economic system properly described as capitalism. There is no such system. The words capital and capitalism are very modern. One of the earliest definitions of capital, and one of the very best, is that made by McCulloch in 1825.[3] He defined capital as the accumulation of the products of previous labor. It would not be easy to find a clearer or more satisfactory definition. Capitalism, used as the name of a system of economic organization, is very recent indeed. It did not come into anything like common use earlier than sixty years ago. To speak bluntly, capital is not the foundation of any economic system whatsoever. Capital is the product of social, economic and

[2] Arnold Ruge und Karl Marx, *Deutsch-Französische Jahrbücher* (Paris, 1844), p. 75.

[3] McCulloch, John R., *Political Economy* (London: 1825), Vol. II, p. 73.

political liberty. Therefore it is liberty, the underlying principle, which is at stake and not capital, which is only the product of liberty. Capital is what remains to the worker by hand or brain when he has met the cost of his work and of his livelihood. Every worker, by hand or by brain, becomes a capitalist the moment he saves anything. When he puts his savings in a bank or in an annuity or in an insurance policy, he is co-operating with those of his fellow workmen who have also become capitalists, to provide the means to multiply work through co-operation with others who, like himself, have made good use of their liberty. The present-day popular use of capitalism as a term of contempt and derision is absolutely without historic or economic justification. This term was seized upon by the enemies of social, economic and political liberty because of its presumed unpopularity and it has been used with increasing violence and vehemence as a weapon of attack against liberty for a full generation. It is the favorite weapon of the Communists and radical Socialists and should be recognized as such. While they profess to be fighting capital, what they are really fighting is that which makes capital possible, namely liberty, whether social, economic or political. They are shrewd enough not to attack liberty directly for they know full well how disastrous to themselves the consequences of such an attack would be among any English-speaking people.

It is also an illusion to assert that all wealth is produced by labor alone. A cursory reading of history and observation of any uncivilized tribe, whether ancient or modern, should dispel this illusion at once. Mere labor may gain a livelihood, but little or nothing more.

It is intelligence which produces wealth. This intelligence may guide the hand of the bricklayer or that of the house painter or that of the locomotive engineer or that of the draftsman, but in each case it is intelligence, and not the mere physical operation of the human hand, which adds to the possessions of mankind. It is this same intelligence, working in a different sphere of expression, which makes possible the poet, the artist, the orator or the statesman. All of these, whether their work be done primarily with their hands or not, have much more in common than is ordinarily understood.

It is also to be borne in mind that when the words Socialism and Communism first came into use a century ago, they described states of mind and ideals, not economic institutions. The state of mind and ideals of Socialism, in particular, were praiseworthy in high degree. They meant that men were not to give themselves over to a life of selfishness and one of purely self-concern, but that they were to think of their fellow men, their companions in the state, their happiness and their well-being. These ideals meant also that gain-seeking, however useful, practical and necessary within proper limits, must not be permitted to pass from under the control of moral principles and the moral sense. So long as Socialism represented all this, it was holding a high and fine ideal before the lovers of liberty. This ideal was one which lovers of liberty could aim to achieve without any surrender of liberty or without any overthrow of the historic institutions which liberty had brought into existence. It was when Socialism passed from being a state of mind and an ideal, to a program of social, economic and political action that it became dangerous to man's highest interests. When it came to mean a plan of public action which substituted compulsion for liberty and strict regimentation for freedom, then Socialism lost its power to inspire and became the symbol of a spirit and type of social, economic and political reaction which would sooner or later check liberty in grievous fashion and perhaps destroy it forever. In other words, the aims of Socialism achieved under the protection and on the basis of the principles of liberty offer a program of hope and progress, while the aims of Socialism achieved through the denial or destruction of liberty are a fatal blow to all that is highest and best in human nature.

It is just because these fundamental and underlying facts and principles are not understood and interpreted that there is so much unclear thinking and unwise action in respect to the labor problem. Every one in his right mind sympathizes with him whom we describe familiarly as the under-dog. Every one in his right mind must wish that health, comfort and happiness be the reward of all those who work, whether with hand or with brain, and that no stone be left unturned to bring this about. The notion that one man may oppress his fellow man for his own gain or glory is immoral. It violates all sound principles of human life and conduct. The way to get rid of it, however, is not by the destruction of any one of the fundamental principles by which human life and human conduct have so long been guided and inspired. The way to get rid of it is by the education of public opinion which, however slow and halting, is the one sure basis for sound and continuing public action. To this may properly be added such legal enactments as wise discretion and large-minded human sympathy find to be really helpful and in consonance with the underlying principles of a sound democratic order.

The first step to be taken in relation to these matters is to make it perfectly plain by statute what forms of agitation and organized activity will be permitted by the public when undertaken either by organized employees or their employers, and what forms will not be permitted. When this vitally important step shall have been taken, it will then be proper to study how best, whether by compulsory incorporation or otherwise, organizations of employees or of employers may be held and made responsible for any action in violation of law. Enlightenment, fair dealing and education can do much, but while human nature remains as it is there will be need of the authority of enforceable law to protect the public from injury and outrage.

It is unfortunately the obvious fact that wage-workers in this country are quite innocently being exploited on a large scale by those whom we have come to describe as racketeers. Nothing is doing so great damage to the interests of the wage-worker as this exploitation. His sympathies, his emotions and his fears are played upon. He is compelled to take action in which he does not believe and to make payments which he does not desire to make, under the threat of denunciation or persecution for disloyalty to his fellow wage-workers. Not only hundreds but thousands of wage-workers who have had no desire whatever to lay down their tools have been compelled by their so-called leaders to engage in strikes under the guise of promoting the interests of wage-workers, while all that was really at stake was the glorification of these unworthy leaders and the satisfaction of their thirst for power. The truth of this statement is demonstrated by the frequency with which strikes are organized and called when the wage-workers themselves are either entirely satisfied with the conditions under which they are at work or would be able quickly to adjust any differences with their employers through conference or arbitration.

A clear illustration of this is found in some recent happenings in the City of New York. Some months ago pickets paraded not only for days but for many weeks in front of certain buildings, carrying signs saying that workmen of a particular trade were on strike and that their employers were unfair to organized labor. In at least two cases where this picketing was carried on for months there was no strike whatsoever, nor any threat of strike. When the pickets—who had not themselves been employed in the buildings which they picketed— were asked why they were picketing, their answer was that they had been told to do so by the executive officer of their local union. When asked whether they were aware that there was no strike of workers in the building which they were picketing, the pickets replied that they knew nothing about it but were simply carrying out their orders. Pressed for a statement as to what wage conditions their union asked, they named a figure which, if accepted by the employers, would have reduced the annual wage of each of the wage-workers in the trade in question by $256. This reduction the employers had no intention whatever of making or of being forced to make. This picketing went on until it came to an end because of its own ridiculous absurdity.

Public opinion has been shocked, and justly so, by the amazing revelations of the type of racketeering carried on in the County of New York which have been made by Special Prosecutor Dewey in his most able and successful effort to protect the interests of the public and of the wage-worker alike from exploitation by the racketeering of those who call themselves organizers of labor. These racketeers are aided in turn by the cowardice of those holders of public office who, fearing the antagonism of what they call the labor vote, refuse to protect the interests of the public, as they have sworn to do, by the enforcement of law. One does not know whether to denounce more emphatically these timorous office holders or the racketeers who make use of the hopes and ambitions of the wage-worker, as well as of the sympathy of the general public for the wage-worker, in order to gain for themselves power which comes in part from the control of the unaccounted expenditure of large sums of money and in part from the control over the conduct of an industry which would follow upon the granting of their excessive demands.

Within the limits of practical possibility, the shortening of the hours of labor, the increase of monetary wages and salaries and the provision for security in case of illness or dependent old age, are highly desirable, indeed necessary, as much in the interest of the general public as in that of the wage-workers themselves who are to be directly affected. The practical problem is how to bring about these desirable results without permitting economic war at the cost of the general public or the exploitation of the organized wage-workers by those who profess to be their representatives and leaders. The development of collective bargaining is sound and its results admirable if it is participated in by those and only those—or their chosen representatives—who are affected by its results. No wage-worker should be compelled to join in collective bargaining if he does not wish to do so, nor should he be allowed to suffer at the hands either of his fellow workers or of his employers because he prefers to hold himself aloof from any compulsory organization. That is why the so-called closed shop is not only undesirable, but highly inconsistent with any doctrine of personal or economic liberty. As a matter of fact, the advocates of the closed shop, while among the most violent denunciators of Fascism, are alert and eager to practice Fascism at the very first opportunity to do so. There is no more reason why a citizen of the United States should be required, in order to find opportunity for employment, to enroll himself as a member of a trade union, than why he should be compelled to join a given political party, a given church, a given Masonic lodge, or a given debating society.

What, then, are the first steps which should be taken by the public and its government to lessen the likelihood of industrial war and to limit such war when it does break out, so that the public damage will be the least possible? For answer to this question one need not look to the policies and experience of any totalitarian state. The methods by which a totalitarian state would seek to deal with the matter are not only inconsistent with democracy but highly offensive to it. Marked progress has been made, however, both in Sweden and in Denmark, toward solving this fundamental problem. But the most important action from the point of view of the people of the United States is that which was taken by the government of Great Britain following the disastrous general strike of 1926, when it enacted the Trade Disputes and Trade Unions Act of 1927. The drafting and enactment of this statute called for both courage and vision, neither of which, fortunately, was lacking. The title of the statute is, "An Act to declare and amend the law relating to trade disputes and trade unions, to regulate the position of civil servants and persons employed by public authorities in respect of the membership of trade unions and similar organizations, to extend Section 5 of the Conspiracy and Protection of Property Act, 1875, and for other purposes connected with the purposes aforesaid."

The Act proceeds in simple language to define illegal strikes and lockouts; to provide for the protection of persons refusing to take part in illegal strikes or lockouts; to prevent intimidation; to provide that no member of a trade union shall be required to make contribution to the political fund of a trade union; to establish regulations as to civil servants and their membership in organizations of which the primary object is to influence or affect the remuneration or conditions of employment of its members; to forbid local and other public authorities from making it a condition of employment or of continuance in employ of any person that he shall or shall not be a member of a trade union; and finally, to restrain the application of funds of trade unions in contravention of the terms of this Act.

The provisions of this remarkable Act invite and well repay most careful study. While the enactment of this statute was strongly opposed by the Labor Party in the House of Commons, it has been neither repealed nor amended during the ten years following its enactment, although the Labor Party has been in control of the government for part of that time.

The time has come for the enactment of similar legislation in the United States. If properly drafted and considered solely from the viewpoint of the public interest, this legislation may well prove to be a Magna Carta for the wage-worker, whether organized or unorganized, in that it will open the way for him to free himself from exploitation and control by the racketeers. It will help bring to an end the practice of using the public sympathy for those who work as a means of inflicting quick and grave damage upon the innocent public itself.

An indication of what is likely to happen may be found in the important bill (Number 346) introduced into the Assembly of the Legislature of the State of New York on January 25, 1937, by Mr. Wadsworth of Livingston County, and in that introduced into the House of Representatives at Washington on April 5, 1937 (H.R. 6148), by Mr. Hoffman of Michigan. The bill of Mr. Wadsworth is entitled:

An Act providing for annual reports by unions, associations and organizations of employees for the protection of its members employed in private enterprise in this state, to provide information to its members and to the public with respect to its activities, authorizing such unions, associations and organizations to submit suggested legislation for the relief of unemployment and providing for certain other matters incidental thereto.

The bill introduced by Mr. Hoffman is entitled:

A Bill to provide for the registration of labor organizations having members engaged in interstate or foreign commerce and to impose duties upon such labor organizations and the members thereof and to impose liability for unlawful acts upon such organizations and the members thereof, and for other purposes.

The reading of these two proposed acts of legislation will make it plain that the minds of some, at least, of the people's legislative representatives are moving along sound and helpful lines, not in a spirit of animosity or antagonism toward the wage-worker, but quite the contrary. It is the highest interests of the wage-worker which these two proposed statutes have in view, and those highest interests are identical with the interests of the public as a whole. It is the American habit, when a new emergency of any kind arises, to propose to enact a law. This is all very well so far as it goes, but it must not be forgotten that any law affecting human conduct which is either behind public opinion or too much in advance of it, will neither be respected, obeyed nor enforced. It will simply become one more source of contempt for law and neglect of it. Therefore it is of highest importance that in proceeding to formulate public policy in respect to any aspect of the labor problem, public opinion be carefully studied before any new enactment is proposed.

At the present time, it would seem to be quite obvious that public opinion will not countenance what are called

sit-down strikes, or sympathetic strikes in industries
other than that directly affected by a dispute between
employer and employee, or strikes in breach of an existing agreement as to collective bargaining or labor relations, or strikes called without a vote by secret ballot
of the members of the organization immediately concerned, or strikes designed or calculated to coerce the
government, whether local, state or national, either directly or by inflicting hardship and damage upon the
citizens of any community. All these acts should be
made, and in my judgment can now be made, illegal
and the law against them enforced, because it will be
upheld by public opinion. At the same time, any law
of this kind must be so carefully drafted that it will in
no wise limit the freedom of the individual worker or
of the group to which he may belong in endeavoring
within the limits of the law to improve the conditions
under which he works, whether physical or monetary.

When so much shall have been done, it will still be
necessary to make certain that the labor organizations
themselves can be held responsible for their acts. The
shortest and quickest way in which to accomplish this
is to provide that these labor organizations shall be incorporated and required to make reports at stated intervals of their financial operations. It is quite impossible
to avoid establishing these policies if we really propose
to bring order out of the existing chaos and to develop
a situation in which the condition of the wage-worker
may be steadily and satisfactorily improved.

It must be repeated again and again that the strike
is a form of war and there is as much reason to find ways
and means of preventing it as to find ways and means

to prevent military war between nations. Beginning with the first Hague Conference of 1899, the public opinion of the civilized world has turned to arbitration of differences between nations as the first and most practical step toward preventing the appeal to armed force. Precisely the same principle applies to that economic war of which the strike is the method of attack. Samuel Gompers, who was for nearly forty years the most effective and vigorous head of the American Federation of Labor, wrote the exact truth in these words:

The causes of strikes can largely be eliminated by the organization of working people into bona fide trade unions and by the organization of the employers, followed by provisions for chosen representatives to sit around the table and there discuss and determine the problems of industry, transportation, of standards of life and work and service. It is something not widely understood, that industrial agreements reached by negotiations between the organized workers and organized employers are a real product of industry, developed through experience and experimentation, unrestricted and competent to adjust themselves to the growth of the industry out of which they have developed.[4]

In order to accomplish this end, both employees and their employers must be right-minded and fair toward each other, no matter how differently they may at any moment view the problem which then presents itself. What forces violence, the strike, is either stubbornness and unfairness on the part of the employer or ambition for power or personal advantage on the part of those who organize and lead the strike.

[4]Gompers, Samuel, *Seventy Years of Life and Labor* (New York: E. P. Dutton & Co., 1925), Vol. II, pp. 149–150.

Just now there are strongly supported efforts to introduce a new and difficult element into the labor problem through the enactment of legislation, nation-wide in its application, giving authority to an official public agency to regulate wages and the hours of labor. It is hard to understand how any proposal of this kind, however well meant or however carefully drafted, can fail to make new and possibly dangerous trouble. In a territory which stretches from the Atlantic to the Pacific and from Canada to the Gulf of Mexico, conditions of population, of climate, of soil and of livelihood are so widely different that it is almost impossible to conceive of a nation-wide regimentation of any form of industry which would not raise many more problems than it could possibly solve. Any attempt at legislation of this kind throws away one of the greatest advantages of the federal form of government, which is that local governmental authority, that of the constituent states, can be called upon to deal with questions of this kind in a spirit of neighborly understanding of what those conditions are, without attempting to put them all into a straitjacket that must be worn alike by the citizens of Massachusetts and of Arizona, of Pennsylvania and of Montana, of Michigan and of Florida. Nothing will cause the federal form of government to crack and break more certainly or more quickly than any attempt at a form of nation-wide regimentation of any personal or group activity which forms part of the life of the people. One would have thought that the history of the Eighteenth Amendment should have taught its lesson, but apparently it has not done so. Surely the sound and American way in which to solve this problem is to proceed to secure state legislation which shall be as uniform as conditions demand and permit, and then to supplement this state legislation by that amount of federal control which may be necessary to make the plan work as every right-minded man would desire.

Plainly, we come back again and again to the fundamental struggle between ordered liberty and regimentation, between economic peace and constant resort to economic war. One of the curious anomalies is that the most vigorous and persistent advocates and supporters of strikes in all their aspects, however disastrous, are those reactionary radicals who so ardently profess their love of peace and their hatred of war of any kind between nations for any purpose. In other words, these reactionary radicals are opposed to all war except that which they themselves desire to make. Whether this be looked upon as tragic or as comic is a matter of taste, but it is a fact of common knowledge and of constant demonstration.

The conclusions are plain. They are, first, that there must quickly be legislation, both state and federal, which shall protect the public from that economic war, particularly when organized and brought about by leaders of labor organizations who are in all essentials racketeers. The British Trade Disputes and Trade Unions Act points the way. When so much shall have been done, it remains then, by formal action, both state and federal, to make the members of labor organizations fully responsible as American citizens for their acts either as individuals or as members of a corporation. The absence of this legal liability, although any advance toward it has been strongly opposed by labor leaders, is really a distinct damage to the interests of the wage-workers. Mr. Justice Brandeis, more than thirty years ago and long before his appointment to be a Justice of the Supreme Court of the United States, used these highly significant words:

This practical immunity of the unions from legal liability is deemed by many labor leaders a great advantage. To me it appears to be just the reverse. It tends to make officers and members reckless and lawless, and thereby to alienate public sympathy and bring failure upon their efforts. It creates on the part of the employers, also, a bitter antagonism, not so much on account of lawless acts as from a deep-rooted sense of injustice, arising from the feeling that while the employer is subject to law, the union holds a position of legal irresponsibility.[5]

More recently, the present Secretary of Labor in the President's Cabinet said this:

If labor's rights are defined by law and by government, then certain obligations will of course be expected of wage earners, and it is for the public interest that those obligations should be defined by labor itself, and that such discipline as is necessary should be self-imposed and not imposed from without. This is the basis of all professional codes of ethics in modern society. . . . There are many signs at the present time . . . that as labor gains status in the community it also imposes upon itself those rules of discipline and self-government necessary for the maintenance of that status.[6]

These are wise words.

[5]Brandeis, Louis D., "The Incorporation of Trade Unions," *Green Bag*, January, 1903, Vol. 15, p. 13.
[6]Perkins, Frances, "A National Labor Policy," *Annals of the American Academy of Political and Social Science*, March, 1936, Vol. 184, pp. 1–2.

The industrial problem in all its aspects has become world-wide. Its particular form may appear differently in this country or in that, but the underlying conditions are everywhere the same. This is why the industrial problem lies at the very root of every practical movement to restore and to maintain world prosperity, as well as to establish and to maintain international peace. It is becoming obvious that in the United States this industrial problem is to fashion and to control the political differences and policies of the years immediately before us.

The existing political parties, Republican and Democrat, came into existence in their present form immediately following the Civil War. For a number of years past, it has been increasingly plain that these parties no longer represent save in name, the same underlying differences of political thought and purpose as was originally the case. The two party names have great sentimental appeal and many proud memories, but they are no longer really significant in the way that they once were. At the present time, both of the historic American parties are completely wrecked by reason of the fact that the commanding industrial problem cannot be fitted into either of their traditional programs and, as a matter of fact, it divides their membership from top to bottom. The time has therefore come when, if the economic life of the people is to be dealt with constructively and intelligently by government, then the party division of the immediate future must represent different and opposing ways of developing the nation's economic resources and of preventing economic strife, whether between employers and employed, or between industrialists and agriculturists or between our own people and those of any other nation.

With this in mind, the line of division between the political parties is clearly indicated. The one party, which might properly be called Constitutional Liberal, would aim to deal with economic questions and to solve economic problems as they arise in a spirit of liberal, forward-facing and constructive statesmanship, but within the limits of the principles underlying the Constitution of the United States and its classic Bill of Rights. That Constitution remains open to amendment by the people themselves should it prove at any time to be not sufficiently elastic in its interpretation to meet the really important needs of the moment.

The opposition party, which would probably wish to be called Progressive, should properly be designated as Reactionary Radical, since it would, on the other hand, proceed to deal with the economic questions of the time without any restriction whatever arising from the American form of government. This Radical party, whatever its name, would be reactionary in fact because its aim would be to pull up by the roots everything that exists, to destroy the gains of centuries of economic, social and political development, and to insist upon regimentation by government as a substitute for ordered and constructive liberty. The spokesmen of this Radical party would in words attack Fascism, but in fact they would exceed Fascism in their zeal for control of individual difference and achievement of any kind.

Were the American people to organize themselves into two such parties, the air would be quickly cleared of many misconceptions and the public would soon come to understand the fundamental differences of thought and of policy that were involved in the party contest. As party names and party divisions now exist, this is not the case, and that of itself is a very serious matter. In a democracy there is no place for a Labor party any more than for a Banker's party or a Farmer's party or a School Teacher's party or a party bearing the name and trying to serve the interests of any other special economic or social group. Democracy implies equality of opportunity and democratic government can only be carried on in accordance with definite underlying principles of thought and action and not with a view to the domination or advantage of any group or class in the population.

The sooner this party reorganization comes and the sooner the American people align themselves on the basis of fundamental principles which apply to present-day conditions, the sooner shall we increase the effectiveness of our government in all its parts and the more adequately serve the interests of the entire people. In no case will the American people countenance the indefinite continuance of any part of their citizenship being deprived of that opportunity and that reward of their honest endeavor which are essential for any one who bears the name American.

V

THE ENGLISH–SPEAKING PEOPLES

An address delivered at the Annual Meeting
of the Pilgrims of the United States, New York
January 26, 1938

THE ENGLISH–SPEAKING PEOPLES

By fortunate coincidence, this day of the annual meeting of the Pilgrims of the United States is Australia Day. In every part of that vast continent on the other side of the world, so little known to most of us, there is being celebrated today the one hundred and fiftieth anniversary of the first raising of the British flag upon that continent. It was raised by Captain Phillip on January 26, 1788, and Australia today is making full recognition of that fact in its own worthy manner. We are particularly happy to greet as a guest at our board the Official Secretary for Australia in the United States, Mr. David M. Dow.

This coincidence is interesting because of what it suggests. Recall for a moment what was happening in the world when the British flag was first placed on the continent of Australia at a spot which is now included in the great city of Sydney. Frederick the Great of Prussia, who had just died, had started that kingdom on its conquering path, which it followed until a climax was reached nearly a century later under the guidance of Bismarck. The rumblings of the beginnings of the French Revolution were plainly to be heard. George III was still upon the English throne, and the movements of opinion and of political, social and economic policy that were so greatly to change the whole form of the British Government and British life during the next half-century were already in full evidence. The voices of Burke, of Fox and of the younger Pitt were to be heard all over the English-speaking world. On this side of the Atlantic, the American people were at that very moment debating in their several state conventions whether they would ratify the Federal Constitution which had been agreed upon and submitted for ratification by the Constitutional Convention held at Philadelphia in 1787. Moreover, in the field of letters, in the field of science, in the field of music and in the field of the fine arts there were extraordinary developments going forward in every civilized land.

Today we think, and justly, that we ourselves are living at a critical time in the world's history when vast changes, not all of which we understand or appreciate, are taking place all about us. But we must not forget that there have been similar happenings in the world before, and one of those times is that which is suggested by the fact that this is Australia Day.

How little we know of that continent, even after one hundred and fifty years! Apparently its existence had been suspected long before it was really discovered. Doubtless rumors had come from China and other parts of the Orient that down in the South Sea there was a great body of land, but the early Dutch, Portuguese and Spanish explorers who appear to have touched upon one or another of the points on its western shore had no conception of what Australia was or what it might be found to be. It was probably Captain Cook himself, approaching it from the east, who first gained some conception of the fact that here was a great body of unknown and unsettled land. When you read its very names, those of its provinces, New South Wales, Victoria, Queensland, and of its cities, Sydney, Melbourne, Brisbane, Adelaide—the name of the wife of William IV—and Perth, you immediately get an accurate knowledge of the dates when these settlements were made, when these provinces were organized and when these cities and towns began to form and to strike root.

How many of us know that the area of Australia is just about equal to the area of the whole United States? How many of us know that the population now to be found in that vast area is only almost exactly that of the city of New York? New Zealand, which is some twelve hundred miles away, has an area twice the size of the state of New York, occupied by a population about equal to that of the Borough of the Bronx or the Borough of Queens. If you ask for an explanation of these vast areas with their relatively small populations, you find it in facts which are not ordinarily familiar to us. You find it in the geology, the topography and the climate, which combine to restrict to relatively narrow portions of those vast areas the regions which are easily open to settlement, to agriculture and to industry.

This great continent is a part, an integral part, of the family of English-speaking nations. We owe it to ourselves to know much more about it than we do at present. It has already begun to produce both in prose, in poetry and in the drama. Excellent historical writing is being done by Australian pens. The greatest scientist of the generation just closing was Lord Rutherford, who was born in New Zealand. Gilbert Murray, outstanding classical scholar, Regius Professor of Greek in the University of Oxford, is a native of Sydney. It is plain then that this distant member of our English-speaking family has something to say to us, something to tell us and an invitation to offer us.

One of the most pressing necessities of our times is that these English-speaking peoples of ours should know a great deal more about each other than they have yet come to do. Of course we have a considerable body of English, of Americans, of Canadians, of Australians, who travel, who read, who reflect and who have a more or less accurate and complete knowledge of the intellectual life, the literature, the science, the art and the institutions of other parts of the English-speaking world than their own; but the number of these is, relatively speaking, infinitesimal. We have not yet reached the great body of the population of any of these countries with the information needed to enable them to appreciate and to understand the mode of thinking, the aspiration, the reflection and the historical experiences of their brothers and sisters in other English-speaking lands.

Down to 1776 we Americans have precisely the same history of politics and of literature as have all other branches of the English-speaking race. Divergence began at that time. It has long been customary in our schools and colleges to teach much of English history and of English literature—not all that should be taught, not as usefully perhaps and as profitably as it should be taught, but still much has been taught. On the other hand, in the board schools of Great Britain there has been substantially no instruction whatever in the history, the literature and the institutions of the United States. A vigorous attempt is now making with official assistance and widespread interest in Great Britain to remedy that defect. You realize, I am sure, that I am not speaking of the so-called intellectual element of the population. I am not speaking of university professors and university students. I am speaking of the great mass of the population enrolled in what we call public schools and in what in England are called board schools. These young people usually know the name of Washington and in a general way that for which Washington stood. They know often the name of Lincoln and that for which Lincoln stood, but beyond that they have hardly any accurate knowledge of the history, the thought, the literature and the institutions which the English-speaking people have built here in the United States of America. What is now being done at the instance of the Carnegie Endowment for International Peace, with strong support in Great Britain itself, will remedy that defect and fill that gap. It is a safe prediction that in a few years the great mass of students, millions in number, in the board schools of Great Britain will be having a full year of instruction in American history, American literature and American institutions. They will thereby get a far better understanding and appreciation than they have heretofore had of what is taking place on this side of the Atlantic. It is not enough for our fellow English-speaking peoples to know of Washington and of Lincoln. They must be brought to know the meaning of the names Hamilton and Jefferson, the Adamses and Madison, Webster and Clay, Hamilton Fish and Elihu Root, as well as the names of our several presidents of the United States. They must know what contribution each one of these has made not only to the public life of the United States and to the building of our institutions but what contribution each has made to the thought and institutional life of the whole English-speaking world. Our American literature has been rich indeed, much richer in fact than that of any other country which is as young as ours. England has good knowledge, better than one would ordinarily think, of Emerson, of Poe, of Walt Whitman and of Lowell. The knowledge of Lowell is the outgrowth largely of his residence as American Minister in London and of his many contacts with the intellectual life of the English people during his time of service. There remains a great body of literary and historical reading which has yet to be taught and interpreted.

Just so we on our side of the Atlantic owe it to ourselves to make sure that the great mass of our population know the meaning of the great names in the history of Great Britain during the century and a half since our own Constitution was adopted and we became a separate and independent sovereign nation. It is most important that we should not bring our knowledge of England to an end with the names of Burke and Fox and Pitt. We should come on down through Castlereagh and Melbourne and Peel and Russell and Palmerston to Disraeli and Gladstone and Rosebery and Salisbury and Balfour and Asquith. It is imperative that we know what each of those leaders of opinion stood for and what service he rendered to his people.

Then, too, during the well-named Victorian era English literature and English history were immeasurably rich. In poetry, in prose, in history, in philosophy and in science there were constant contributions made of greatest importance. We must bring the great mass of our population to some understanding of all this. It will not be the understanding of the intellectual leader or of the specialist, but the understanding and appreciation of the ordinary citizen of what have been the means of expression that their fellows in the other parts of the English-speaking world have developed and used. It will be an understanding of how they have recorded their aspirations and their reflections. That understanding will be worth all the political policies in the world in bringing us into closer co-operation and fuller understanding. Great populations which have learned to think alike and to feel alike do not have to be taught how to act alike. Their action becomes the automatic reflection of their aspiration and their feeling. As the world grows older and these linguistic differences become more striking and more marked—as they certainly do—we point to our tongue and its achievements and we find nothing in history like it save in ancient Greece. How small that was in comparison with the hundreds of millions that our poets and essayists and critics and dramatists and orators reach day by day not only in Great Britain, not only in Canada, in India, in Australia, in New Zealand, in the Union of South Africa, but in these United States and in every part of the world where the influence of the United States penetrates.

Believe me, my fellow Pilgrims, there is a real task here, a task not to be put in terms of political action, a task not to be put in terms of economic policies, a task not to be stated in terms of social reconstruction. It is a task of education in the largest sense of that word, and yet it is not technically education. It is a task of bringing human beings to a more close and mutual understanding of each other through a knowledge and appreciation of their mode of expression and of the monuments which they have erected to their ideals.

Today, when Australia, at that great distance from us all and with its limitations, geologic and climatic, can begin to send around the world contributions to this intellectual life and to its expression, what a new inducement and inspiration that fact is. It stirs us to carry on as rapidly as we may and as thoroughly as we can this interpenetration of the English-speaking peoples through a grasp on the masses of each of them of what their literary, their artistic and their scientific expression mean when applied to their nature, to their ideals and to their views of life. It is a great task, it is a great call to the English-speaking people of today and tomorrow. Let us make sure that we answer it.

VI

THE BELL IS RINGING

An address delivered at the 186th Commencement
of Columbia University
June 4, 1940

THE BELL IS RINGING

A century and a half ago, as his world-famous *History of the Decline and Fall of the Roman Empire* drew to its close, Edward Gibbon wrote these remarkable words concerning that which is called "the greatest, perhaps, and most awful scene in the history of mankind":

The various causes and progressive effects are connected with many of the events most interesting in human annals: the artful policy of the Caesars, who long maintained the name and image of a free republic; the disorders of military despotism; the rise, establishment, and sects of Christianity; the foundation of Constantinople; the division of the monarchy; the invasion and settlements of the Barbarians of Germany and Scythia; the institutions of civil law; the character and religion of Mahomet; the temporal sovereignty of the popes; the restoration and decay of the Western empire of Charlemagne; the crusades of the Latins in the East; the conquests of the Saracens and Turks; the ruin of the Greek empire; the state and revolutions of Rome in the middle age.

What will the Gibbon of five hundred years hence have to say concerning those happenings which are now shaping the history of the modern world in this twentieth century? From the time of Magna Carta, which is more than seven hundred years old, and more particularly from the time of the political revolutions of the seventeenth and eighteenth centuries, the process of nation-building on this earth has gone forward with steadily increasing regard for sound principles of public morals and for the welfare, the happiness and the civil, economic and political liberty of the people. Much surely remained to be done, for wars were certainly frequent enough, and anything approaching perfection was still a long way off; but progress was steadily making. Everywhere the intellectual leaders of the world had confidence in the future.

During the nineteenth century, however, seeds of discontent had been sown which, as that century drew to its end, were seen to bear obvious and unfortunate fruits in the conduct of men. The well-established ideals of civil liberty and moral purpose, in accordance with which each individual was given opportunity to do his best to render service to his fellow men in terms of industry, of character and of intelligence, were undermined and sought to be displaced by a wholly false and reactionary conception of the social order, which divided it into permanent and antagonistic classes. These classes, it was asserted, had competing and conflicting aims, thereby inviting the rule of force instead of the rule of reason and of morals. As the twentieth century advanced and the seeds of this false doctrine continued to bear fruit, it began to affect the policies of governments, and a world of free and co-operating nations, whether great or small, was turned into a world of jealous and competing nations, each making colossal expenditure to arm itself in preparation for an ultimate appeal to force. By words and policies of astounding insincerity, all offensive aims were displaced by those which claimed to be simply defensive. Declared war began to disappear, and in its stead there came acts of cruel and merciless aggression upon smaller and weaker peoples who were trying to live their own independent and happy lives, to the end that a greater and a stronger nation might, under the impulse of blind and superselfish gain-seeking, immorally increase its authority and strengthen its position at the cost of its neighbors.

This is where the world is today. As a result, the progress of civilization is hanging in the balance, and whether we and our children are to witness another decline and fall of the Roman Empire is something which no man dare yet prophesy with confidence.

What is to be done about it? Is it too late to inform public intelligence and to arouse public feeling to the support and defense of those progressive and liberal institutions which we thought had come to stay and would grow stronger century by century? What would the great English and French liberal leaders and philosophers of the eighteenth and nineteenth centuries have had to say about such a state of affairs? What would the builders of the American Republic have thought of it? Imagine Washington and Hamilton and Jefferson and Madison and Webster and Lincoln faced by such a crisis as that which now confronts us! Would they not, each and all, have been dazed and stupefied by the spectacle of millions of armed men marching about in support of autocracy and the extension of its area of conquest in a world which had accepted the Petition of Right and the Bill of Rights in England, the Déclaration des Droits de l'Homme in France, and the Bill of Rights of the Federal Constitution of the United States, as statements of definite and lasting principles upon which world civilization and world progress would rest?

It is for this generation and for that which will soon follow to give answer to these questions. Vast and far-reaching forces of human emotion, human ambition and human greed cannot be lightly dealt with or waved aside with some magic formula. They must be met, conquered and suppressed by calm and reasoned intelligence, and the call is for all men in every land. No one can be isolated from this colossal struggle. Where despots have gained unprecedented authority, those over whom they are so cruelly ruling must unhorse them. Where the forms of civil, religious and political liberty still exist, they must be strengthened and given new power over the hearts as well as over the minds of men. Faith must not be lost, and courage must not be lacking. The call is for every civilized human being who believes in justice, in liberty and in public morals. The bell is ringing!

VII

COLUMBIA UNIVERSITY IN THIS WORLD CRISIS

An address delivered at a
General Assembly of the University Faculties
McMillin Academic Theatre
Columbia University
October 3, 1940

COLUMBIA UNIVERSITY IN THIS WORLD CRISIS

At the opening of this new academic year it is of high importance that we examine and reflect upon the problems which face Columbia University in view of the world crisis which is shaking our historic civilization to its foundations. Our University, founded nearly two hundred years ago as a simple American college, has become with the passing years a powerful public servant in the field of liberty. It has responded to the opportunities and ideals of historic university development, and its place in the intellectual life of the world and in the shaping of public policies, national and international, is now well established.

Because of the present world war, primarily economic but now violently and brutally military as well, this institution at work in the field of liberty is called upon to co-operate with government. The purpose of this co-operation is to strengthen the defenses of our American system of economic, social and political liberty, and to defend them and the republican form of government built upon them from attack having its origin either without or within our own country. This co-operation with government is a service which Columbia has always been willing and quick to offer. The greatest names on its roll became famous through leadership and service in this field of action. Today as Columbia approaches the end of its second century of corporate life, it will not be found wanting in this endeavor.

The appalling war which has now in its grasp practically the whole of Europe and a great part of Asia and of Africa as well, has brought the United States of America face to face with an emergency such as it has never hitherto known. We hope and pray that it may not be our lot to have to take part in the military struggle which is going on, but we are involved, and have been from the beginning, in the economic aspects of that struggle and in the war of ideas and ideals which it represents and reflects. At such a time it is a direct responsibility of the Federal Government under the leadership of the President of the United States to plan quickly and thoroughly for the defense of the nation. Already the President and the Congress have taken far-reaching action on behalf of all of us in order to enable the American people and their government to protect and to defend themselves. At such a time every citizen and every institution of public service built in the field of liberty have a direct responsibility to bear. My purpose in inviting this General Assembly of all the Faculties of the University was to indicate to them in what way the activities of our University can be used in cooperation with the Government to strengthen the nation's defense.

One who reads carefully the history of Europe during the past half-century will recognize that military preparedness, highly important though it be, is but one part of national defense. It is of still higher importance that the people as a whole and their representative institutions understand what it is which they are called upon to defend, and to plan with thoroughness and skill for their part in that defense.

In order that careful and systematic study might be made of this problem, I appointed on July 5 last a University Committee on National Defense constituted of the following members of the University staff in addition to the President of the University:

CARL W. ACKERMAN, Dean of the Faculty of Journalism

CHARLES W. BALLARD, Dean of the College of Pharmacy

JOSEPH W. BARKER, Dean of the Faculty of Engineering

FREDERICK COYKENDALL, Chairman of the Trustees

CONDICT W. CUTLER, JR., Trustee of the University

LESLIE C. DUNN, Professor of Zoölogy

FRANK D. FACKENTHAL, Provost of the University

VIRGINIA C. GILDERSLEEVE, Dean of Barnard College

ROBERT M. HAIG, McVickar Professor of Political Economy

HERBERT E. HAWKES, Dean of Columbia College

GEORGE B. PEGRAM, Dean of the Graduate Faculties

EDMUND A. PRENTIS, Trustee of the University

WILLARD C. RAPPLEYE, Dean of the College of Physicians and Surgeons

LINDSAY ROGERS, Burgess Professor of Public Law

WILLIAM F. RUSSELL, Dean of Teachers College

J. ENRIQUE ZANETTI, Director of Chemical Laboratories

Executive Committee

FRANK D. FACKENTHAL, Chairman

DEANS PEGRAM, HAWKES, BARKER, DR. CUTLER

This representative Committee has been at work for three months upon its problem and has already submitted the first of a series of helpful reports.

It is fortunate that we shall have no difficulty and no difference of opinion in recognizing the true function of a university in this co-operation with government. The aim of a university, of course, is the conservation and extension of knowledge. Therefore, that conservation and extension of knowledge must be undertaken with redoubled vigor in respect to the analysis and understanding of the economic, social and political problems which are involved in this world war and which are creating for the United States the crisis which confronts it. It is fortunate, also, that the Government of the United States in its plans for national defense appreciates this university function. The Government plans the least possible disturbance of the teaching and research work of colleges and universities, and the least possible disturbance of university scholars and students. Indeed, the President of the United States in a public statement has called upon students of all kinds to return to their studies. The Acts recently passed by the Congress recognize this attitude and policy in very considerable degree. Inasmuch as we are confronted in this country and in every other country by emotional outbursts which are quite hysterical in their character and which lead to acts of the utmost cruelty and violence, we must make sure that the scholar uses his opportunity, which is as unique as it is tremendous, to guide public opinion into paths of reason, of reflection and of understanding. It is of the very essence of our national defense that our people as a whole shall understand what it is which they are defending, and that they have this presented to them with calmness, good judgment and full knowledge. In this regard the responsibility of each one of us is very great. We must not ourselves be misled by phrases or formulas, and we must do our best to keep others from being so misled.

We shall no doubt hear much throughout the country in the immediate future in respect to academic freedom. That subject is one which has been discussed several times in my Annual Reports as President of the University, and I need not repeat here what I have said so emphatically in these Reports, particularly in those for the years 1918 and 1935. The policy of Columbia University in this respect has long been well and thoroughly established. As I pointed out in my Report for 1935, for those who are *in statu pupillari* the phrase academic freedom has no meaning whatsoever. That phrase relates solely to freedom of thought and inquiry and to freedom of teaching on the part of accomplished scholars. We all know the history of academic freedom from the time of its first establishment some two centuries ago at Halle and Göttingen. The purpose of academic freedom is to make sure that scholarship and scientific inquiry may advance without being hampered by particular and specific religious or political tenets. Of course, academic freedom has never meant and could not possibly mean in any land the privilege—much less the right—to use the prestige, the authority and the influence of a university relationship to undermine or to tear down the foundations of principle and of practice upon which alone that university itself can rest. University freedom is as important as academic freedom. Before and above academic freedom of any kind or sort comes this university freedom which is the right and obligation of the university itself to pursue its high ideals unhampered and unembarrassed by conduct on the part of any of its members which tends to damage its reputation, to lessen its influence or to lower its authority as a center of sound learning and of moral teaching. Those whose convictions are of such a character as to bring their conduct in open conflict with the university's freedom to go its way toward its lofty aim should, in common sense and self-respect, withdraw of their own accord from university membership in order that their conduct may be freed from the limitations which university membership naturally and necessarily puts upon it. No reasonable person would insist upon remaining a member of a church, for instance, who spent his time in publicly denying its principles and doctrines. There would probably be but very few such cases in all the universities of the world.

It may be taken for granted that the Trustees and the Faculties are prepared to be generous and abundant in understanding in regard to the problems of individual members of the staff or of the student body who are called into full military service. It will be the policy of the University to grant leave of absence without salary to University officers who are called, and I shall recommend to the Trustees that in order to protect the ultimate retiring allowances of such officers the University should assume in the case of those who have already undertaken Teachers Insurance and Annuity Association contracts, to meet both of the 5 per cent contributions called for by those contracts.

Students called to the colors will likewise be given leave of absence and no student in good standing will incur loss of tuition fees through entrance into full-time military service during the academic year. The proper officers of the University will make an equitable arrangement of credit to such students. Wednesday, October 16, will be an academic holiday in order that both officers and students affected by the provisions of the Selective Training and Service Act of 1940 may have ample opportunity to register.

Already the University Committee on National Defense has organized activities of military usefulness for the voluntary participation of students and has still others in prospect for the academic year 1941–42. That Committee will welcome suggestions from any member of the University, whether teacher or student, in relation to matters which fall under its jurisdiction. The special courses and programs which have already been arranged include:

1. a unit for the training of air pilots under the Civil Aeronautics Administration.
2. an Orientation course under the direction of the Department of Civil Engineering, making use of the facilities both at Morningside Heights and at Camp Columbia. This course in military engineering will be given academic credit in Columbia College and in the School of Engineering.
3. In addition, it is hoped that there will shortly be organized a Marine Corps Reserve Training unit which, if established, will lead to a commission as second lieutenant in the Marine Corps Reserves, and will involve one night a week during the academic year and training at Camp Columbia for two periods of six weeks each, following the Sophomore and Junior years.

Attention of students is also called to the opportunity quite likely to be offered in the immediate future by

the Navy Department for training through courses of
Naval Reserve Midshipmen leading to commission as
Ensign in the volunter Naval Reserve.

Undoubtedly, other opportunities will be arranged
in the not distant future.

It is of the highest importance that we all bear in
mind the need which will be most pressing when armed
hostilities come to an end, to undertake once more the
task of laying the foundations for a system of international organization and co-operation for the protection
of the world's prosperity and the world's peace. We
must not be disheartened because of the failure of the
attempts toward this high end which had already been
made. We must resume those attempts with redoubled
vigor and armed with the new knowledge which the
experiences of the last quarter-century have brought us.
Fortunately, we have a statement of ideals and of the
program by which those ideals may be best achieved
in the noteworthy plan agreed upon by the members
of the Conference held at Chatham House, London, in
March, 1935. At that Conference sixty-two of the most
distinguished statesmen and men of affairs in the world,
coming from ten countries including Germany and
Italy, agreed unanimously upon a series of recommendations which were subsequently endorsed by the unanimous vote of the International Chamber of Commerce.
These recommendations constitute a convincing program for world reconstruction. It is upon this world
reconstruction that our eyes must be fixed. It will not
do to sit helplessly by and content ourselves with saying
that no reconstruction is possible, that civilization is on
its way to death and that the world as we and our an-

cestors have known it can never be restored. The temptation to that point of view and that attitude is certainly very great, but it is a temptation to which we simply must not yield. It would not be characteristic of us as American scholars to lose our faith, our hope and our confidence in the ability of mankind to bring ultimate victory to moral principle and the spirit of service over the mad and cruel lust for gain and for power; for that is the essential struggle underneath and behind the economic war. Behind the war of conflicting political doctrines, underneath and behind the war of lust for gain and for domination over one's fellow men, there lies the war between beasts and human beings, between brutal force and kindly helpfulness, between the spirit of gain at any cost and the spirit of service built upon common sense and moral principle. Let there be no doubt where Columbia University stands in this war.

VIII

OUR UNITED STATES IN A
BACKWARD–MOVING WORLD

An address delivered
at the Parrish Memorial Art Museum
Southampton, Long Island
September 1, 1940

OUR UNITED STATES IN A
BACKWARD–MOVING WORLD

The human race is witnessing the greatest and most far-reaching revolution which history records and is in large part under its control. This revolution, which is primarily the outgrowth of economic problems and economic ambitions, has for more than a quarter-century involved the whole world. It took on violent military form with the declaration of war on August 1, 1914. It is that war, checked for a time by an armistice and by a treaty of peace that looked backward instead of forward,[1] which is again raging, and in far more cruel, inhuman and destructive form. It is in every sense of the word a war of real revolution.

Whether it be generally recognized or not, what we call the civilized world, which for seven hundred years has been moving steadily forward in the spirit of liberalism and toward liberalism's high ideals, has now turned suddenly and violently backward. The guidance of reason and of understanding, of moral principle and of religious faith, has been shockingly and cruelly displaced by the rule of brute force. Our literally stupendous achievements in literature, in philosophy, in the arts, in the sciences and in the comforts and conveniences of life count for nothing in the control of

[1]Cf. Bryant, Arthur, *Unfinished Victory* (London: Macmillan & Co., 1940).

national policy and of national conduct, and by far the major portion of the world is now under the rule of brutal compulsion. Such portion of the world as is not in that condition may soon be struggling for its life.

Had any one ventured a generation ago to predict that a great and highly civilized people like the Germans, with their magnificent record of accomplishment and influence in every aspect of the intellectual life, could have been reduced to mere blind and unreasoning instruments of torture and of brute force, he would have been thought quite mad. Nevertheless, just that has happened. So appalling a set of conditions and circumstances must be examined with dispassionate care in order that we may have something to guide us in judging what may be the meaning of it all and what will be its possible effect upon that which we Americans hold most dear.

One of the most influential happenings with which we have to deal and which is but little recognized is the effect on public opinion of the outstanding excellence of contemporary journalism, particularly in these United States, and of the world-wide news spread hour by hour through the radio. These powerful agencies, the press and the radio, have substituted information for knowledge. The steady flow of that information which they give so absorbs the attention of tens of millions of human beings that they have no opportunity and little temptation to give to this mass of information that critical interpretation and reflective understanding which might transform it into knowledge. We are therefore, in very large measure, living on the surface of the world's happenings. Few indeed are those who have the capacity and the ability to go beneath that surface and to grasp the real significance of the knowledge which information might, but often does not, involve and convey. It is of vital importance that we learn to look beneath the surface of things.

As a matter of fact, the path which the constructive thought of the world was treading from the beginning of the twentieth century down almost to the outbreak of the World War of 1914–18 was the most hopeful and progressive in all modern history. Signs multiplied that statesmen and the people for whom they spoke had gained the vision of a prosperous, a contented and a peaceful world, organized for the preservation and protection of law and order in a way that would promote all those inspiring ideals which we recognize as the spirit and guide of liberalism.

What happened? Why was this progress, so full of promise and satisfaction, brought suddenly to an end, and why were reactionary and abhorrent forces set loose, to meet with so little effective opposition that they bid fair to control the world for generations and to put it back, as no one of us had ever believed possible, to a condition which is essentially one of barbaric rule by sheer force?

Bluntly, the answer must be that the democracies, foremost among which were France, Great Britain and the United States, showed themselves incompetent and unable to understand the new economic and political forces at work in the world and to co-operate for their control and direction in a manner which would preserve and protect the democratic system of economic, social and political order, as well as those free institutions which had, we thought, been safely and permanently built upon that order. During these critical years the democracies have conspicuously lacked the able, constructive and courageous leadership which was so sorely needed. They were allowed to drift on the shoals of disaster.

Consider for a moment the progress which was making from· 1898 to 1920 in the building of a system of world organization and international co-operation that should control and guide the new economic forces which the Industrial Revolution had set at work. The purpose, of course, was to increase prosperity for all peoples, great and small, and to protect the foundations of international peace through international co-operation. The first note of progress in this movement was struck by the noteworthy rescript appealing for international co-operation to promote peace, issued by the Czar of All the Russias in 1898. Immediately, the progressive and liberal forces of the world rallied to respond to that appeal. It will always be a matter of pride to many of us that the government of the United States took the lead in that great movement for world organization. It was the influence of the American delegation which gave to the first Hague Conference of 1899 the measure of success which it attained. From the speech of President McKinley made at Buffalo on September 5, 1901, containing the striking sentence, so often quoted, "The period of exclusiveness is past," down to the formal declarations by the two great political parties in the presidential campaign of 1920, American opinion showed itself ready to take responsible leadership in guiding the world toward a peaceful solution of all international differences and difficulties. It had grasped the fact that the only possible way to avoid war and to keep out of war was to unite to remove the causes of war. The policies of Presidents Theodore Roosevelt and Taft, of Secretaries of State John Hay and Elihu Root, all reflected and expressed this spirit of world leadership. Then came—as I have often pointed out—the epoch-marking Joint Resolution passed in June, 1910 by both Houses of the American Congress without a single dissenting vote, authorizing the President to begin negotiations with other governments in order to bring about a world organization which would establish and protect peace through the aid of an international police force composed of the combined navies of the world. How many of those who profess to represent public opinion in the United States today have ever heard of that Joint Resolution or know that it was passed without a dissenting vote?

The persistent assertion that the traditional policy of the United States is one of national and international isolation is contrary to every fact in our history. No people in the world has had more intimate, more constant and more influential relationships with other peoples than ourselves. Outstanding and distinguished examples of this international relationship and international influence are Benjamin Franklin, John Adams, Thomas Jefferson, John Jay, John Marshall, John Quincy Adams, Ralph Waldo Emerson and James Russell Lowell. The steady flow of immigration from one European country after another gave to our population long ago the many-sided character and intellectual interest which will always mark the American people.

We required the military co-operation of the people and the army of France in order to win the War of Independence. We found a way to take part in the war between Napoleon and Great Britain in what is called the War of 1812, against the protest of so outstanding a statesman and leader as Daniel Webster. Our country was invaded and public buildings at Washington were burned. When that war came to an end and the Treaty of Ghent was signed, not the slightest reference was made to those matters which had been alleged to have caused America's participation in the war. The War with Mexico was undertaken against the protest of Abraham Lincoln, who as Representative in Congress from the State of Illinois voted against it. The Spanish-American War in 1898 was absolutely unnecessary, and if it had not been insisted upon by the belligerent press, aided by numerous influential leaders of opinion, including Theodore Roosevelt, Cuba would have become free through diplomatic arrangement with Spain and without any armed hostilities whatsoever. The cost to the people of the United States of that unnecessary war is quite appalling, since highly organized and efficient lobbies have provided for a system of pensions to persons whose relation to the war was only nominal, which have already amounted to tens of millions of dollars and will continue yet for a long generation.

Isolation is the last thing of which the American government and the American people can be accused. Millions of American people are day by day and almost hour by hour informed and deeply interested in news from other peoples in every part of the world. No other people manifests a like international interest. American agriculture, American industry, American commerce and American finance have penetrated and influenced the life of every nation on the globe. Moreover, it must not be forgotten that it was an American, Commodore Perry, who in 1852, under the express instructions of President Fillmore, to all intents and purposes discovered Japan and introduced its people to world trade and world relationship.

Unfortunately, the World War of 1914–18 broke before the European nations had been persuaded to accept the proposals of the American government made by President Taft pursuant to the Joint Resolution of 1910. But President Wilson had a great vision, and he offered a system of world organization similar to that proposed by the American Congress, to be effective when the Great War should come to its end. Unhappily, his temperament was such that he permitted personal frictions and dislikes to guide his public statements and his policies in a way which greatly weakened his influence and his leadership. Nevertheless, when the American people chose their President in 1920, they did so having before them the definite pledges of both great political parties to support an agreement among the nations to preserve the peace of the world. The statement contained in the Republican national platform was particularly clear and definite.

It is therefore obvious and of record that the American people were betrayed by the failure of those who were chosen to public office in 1920 to carry out the pledges so definitely made to them. Indeed, it is just at this point that a beginning is to be found for the causes of those appalling happenings which have in twenty years succeeded in revolutionizing so large a portion of the world. It needed the votes of but a very small group of members of the United States Senate to deprive the American people of the safety, the benefit and the world leadership which they had then been pledged. The construction of a world of co-operating nations should then have gone forward under American inspiration and American leadership. Had this been done, we might well be living today in a far different world from that which confronts us.

With this record of promise and with these explicit pledges before us, it may again be pointed out what nonsense it is to speak of our having had a traditional policy of isolation, and of our having no interest in what happens to our fellow men in other lands! The truth is the precise opposite. We had offered leadership to the world, and both political parties had pledged it to the American people. It was the petty politicians at Washington and their shocking disregard of moral and political obligation which threw away the great opportunity which our government had envisaged and of which both political parties had pledged themselves to take advantage. If there be one definite cause, more explicit and more obvious than any other, of the weakness, and it may even be the downfall, of the democracies, it certainly finds expression in this disastrous record of the faithlessness of the small-minded American politician and office-holder, who had in his power for the time being the control of great public policies.

But even so, since a plan of world organization was accepted and entered upon through the establishment of the League of Nations at Geneva, there still seemed opportunity for readjustment of a constructive and progressive character in the field of international relations. But neither the government of France nor the government of Great Britain stood firm on the new platform which had been erected. Both consistently backed and filled and compromised and hesitated, lest some gain-seeking undertaking might be interfered with if the high ends for which the League of Nations had been organized were vigorously and courageously pursued. Nevertheless, under the inspiring leadership of M. Briand, fifteen governments ratified in 1928 the famous Pact of Paris for the renunciation of war as an instrument of national policy, and no fewer than sixty-three governments had signed and ratified this Pact by 1934. Many of us then thought that the end of war was in sight. We little realized the faithlessness of the signatory governments and that they would at once begin to prepare for war on an unprecedented scale of expenditure. Those who, in every land, had been at work for a generation upon these plans to end war by removing the causes of war, were profoundly grieved and shocked as they saw one happening after another which meant the weakening and the eventual tearing down of the structure which was then building.

Even as late as 1931, had there been better understanding and closer co-operation between the governments of some of the democracies, much of the worst which has taken place during the past ten years might never have happened at all. When there was no effective opposition to Japan's invasion of China, then the leaders of Nazi Germany saw no reason why they should not violate their pledges and take possession of the east bank of the Rhine, and the Fascist government of Italy saw no reason why it should not violate its pledges and proceed to the conquest of Ethiopia. Then all barriers were down and the way was opened to the spread of the rule of brute force without the slightest regard for international law, for formal treaties and pledges or for human feeling. What has happened since is so clear and so obvious that it need not be dwelt upon.

The question which presses for an answer is why were these great democracies so incompetent. Why were they so lacking in vision, in courage and in spirit of co-operation? Why was it practicable for a small group of members of the United States Senate to make it impossible for the government of the United States to carry out the pledges which had been made to the American people? What was it which to all intents and purposes paralyzed the governments of France and of Great Britain in their support of the organized society of nations and prevented them from going forward with eagerness and vision on the constructive path of progress which had been pointed out?

The answer in the case of Great Britain may be found succinctly stated in two extraordinary volumes, one of which is a collection of speeches made during the years 1932 to 1938 by Winston Churchill, the present Prime Minister in the government of Great Britain.[2] In the

---

[2]Churchill, Rt. Hon. Winston S., *While England Slept: A Survey of World Affairs*, 1932–1938 (New York: G. P. Putnam Sons, 1938).

Kennedy, John F., *Why England Slept* (New York: Wilfred Funk, 1940).

case of France, political and economic disintegration
had been proceeding at a rapid pace after the death of
Briand, apparently without any effective and constructive leadership to prevent it or to save the great people
of France from the literally appalling fate which has
now overtaken them. Plainly, what France has lacked
in recent years is constructive and courageous moral
and political leadership. The French people have unfortunately been divided into economic and social groups
or classes which contested with each other for the control of the government and which apparently were unable or unwilling to work together for the good of the
French people as a whole and for the glory and honor
of France. The result has astounded the whole world.
Nothing has been more staggering to us than to watch
the forty-two million French people sitting silently and
in coma while a small group of their fellow Frenchmen
signed away not only the government of the Third
Republic, but that great declaration for Liberty, Equality and Fraternity which sounded the note of the French
Revolution a century and a half ago. In each and all of
the democracies there have been and are forces at work
which have gravely interfered with the effectiveness of
these democracies. But it is difficult, if not impossible,
to look upon democracy in France as dead. It is certainly in prison at the moment; but some of us, at least,
will not give up the hope and the faith that it will find
a way to reassert itself in the spirit of the truly great
France of bygone days.

So outstanding a scholar and statesman as the Marquess of Crewe feels that liberalism is everywhere under
an eclipse, and his discussion of the subject is highly

illuminating.[3] He points out that it was in England that the plant of liberalism first took root and that its growth there was slow and intermittent. Party politics played their part sometimes in encouraging liberalism and sometimes in hampering it, but all through the seventeenth and eighteenth centuries it never died down. Then came the day when the French Revolution brought a new atmosphere to Europe and gave to liberalism the new impulse and effectiveness which lasted for a full century. Lord Crewe suggests, however, that liberalism by its very nature lacks cohesion. It promotes and invites differences of opinion and frequently calls upon public opinion to wait and see, rather than to reach a definite conclusion as to action to be immediately taken. The economic influences which began to play so large a part in national and international policy a hundred years ago gave liberalism in England its new opportunity to build itself upon a wider and more effective democratic basis in the shaping of public policy and upon freedom of international trade for the quick promotion of industry and of commerce. Toward the close of the nineteenth century, the weakening of liberalism in England began, and as Lord Crewe points out, its eclipse has continued until this day.

Liberalism in England has certainly been able to stir the mind of the people to influence and to shape legislation in many most important ways, yet there have been forces at work, partly national and partly international, the effect of which has been to limit liberalism's power to guide and to express British public opinion. As Lord

[3]Crewe, Marquess of, "The Eclipse of Liberty," in *The Fortnightly* of London, May, 1940, pp. 474–484.

Crewe states, the present is a most harassing period for liberals, especially for those of the younger generation, who find themselves forced into the political background during their best years and to whom the prospect of political influence and political leadership seems dark indeed. Nevertheless, the closing words of his analysis are these: "But let us conclude with a confident *Sursum corda!*"

It is in this spirit of *Sursum corda* that we Americans must approach the grave problems which stare us in the face. We dare not be discouraged or lacking in faith, for should we be, there would be little left to hope for in the world of today.

It is perfectly evident that all those important problems and policies which we have looked upon as national or domestic are now absorbed into and made part of the world revolution. The ordinary processes of trade and commerce no longer exist, and huge expenditures are making for purposes which we had thought belonged to the past and would never again be necessary. Armament and preparation for military war have become the dominant note in our public life. This means, of course, the diversion of labor and savings from those purposes for which we would wish to use them, to ends which are of necessity wasteful and destructive. Moreover, military war on the stupendous scale on which it is now being waged destroys in a few days the earnings and the savings of men for generations. The disastrous effect of this upon the accumulated wealth of our people will one of these days be quite obvious to every one; but there is no alternative.

Indeed, so absolute and so complete is this revolution

that we are yet unable fully to visualize or understand it. What are we Americans to do in order to protect and to save our own beloved institutions and the historic foundations upon which they rest? We have had ample warning of these problems and dangers, but we have paid little attention to them. It is two generations since Herbert Spencer wrote a famous essay entitled "The Coming Slavery," in which he predicted that tyranny would succeed liberty in England and probably elsewhere. He certainly did not have in mind the totalitarian state in the form in which it is now presented to us by Russia, by Germany and by Italy, but he did have in mind a state of affairs in which the government would control the life and occupations of the people, instead of the people controlling the policies of the government.

If we look frankly and fairly at the facts of our country's history, we cannot fail to see that there have been many signs during the past generation that all was not well with our political thinking and our political policies. So long as we had the leadership of our first six Presidents, each one of whom was an outstanding statesman of competence and of independence, the foundations of our government and political life were unshaken. After their time, however, we entered upon a period of political and partisan struggle the effects of which, while sometimes relatively harmless, were often definitely harmful. Finally, there came the climax of our great Civil War, which apparently was unavoidable. When that was over and the country's unity permanently established, then our problems became primarily economic and social. Whenever we were given opportunity to approach these problems in a spirit of understanding and detachment from group or sectional interest, our public opinion responded to the demands made upon it with reasonably good results. But increasingly, our public opinion and our elected political representatives came under the pressure of closely organized and most persistent minority groups. These minority groups were not concerned with principles nor with the public welfare. They were concerned simply with that particular end upon which they had set their hearts and which appealed either to their imagination or to their personal or group interest. Unfortunately, the activity and influence of these minority groups have become stronger year by year at Washington and at several of our state capitals and today they are a genuine danger to our public welfare. Minority groups are able to exist and to succeed only because the majority group is indifferent and inattentive to them. Every once in a while we have evidence that American public opinion is sound and healthy and can be reached by the highest type of appeal. We have had several instances of this during the past two generations, but in every case grave damage had been done by the minority groups before public opinion effectively asserted itself.

Public opinion is the unseen product of education and practical experience. Education, in turn, is the function, in co-operation, of the family, the church and the school. If the family fails in its guiding influence and discipline and if the church fails in its religious instruction, then everything is left to the school, which is given an impossible burden to bear. It is just this situation which has arisen in the United States during the generation through which we are still passing. In overwhelming proportion, the family has become almost unconscious of its chief educational responsibility. In like manner, the church, fortunately with some noteworthy exceptions, has done the same. The heavy burden put upon the school has resulted in confused thinking, unwise plans of instruction and a loss of opportunity to lay the foundations of true education, the effects of which are becoming obvious to every one. Fundamental discipline, both personal and social, has pretty well disappeared, and, without that discipline which develops into self-discipline, education is impossible.

What are the American people going to do about it? If they do not correct these conditions, they are simply playing into the hands of the advocates of a totalitarian state, for that type of state is at least efficient, and it is astonishing to how many persons efficiency makes stronger appeal than liberty.

Then, too, we have many signs of an incapacity to understand and to interpret liberty, or to distinguish it from license. There is a limit to liberty, and liberty ends where license begins. It is very difficult for many persons to understand this fact or to grasp its implications. If we are to have freedom of speech, freedom of thought and freedom of the press, why should we not be free to say and think and print whatever we like? The answer is that the limit between liberty and license must be observed if liberty itself is to last. To suppose, as many individuals and groups seem to do, that liberty of thought and liberty of speech·include liberty to agitate for the destruction of liberty itself, indicates on the part of such persons not only lack of common sense but lack of any sense of humor. If liberty is to remain, the barrier between liberty and license must be recognized and observed.

In this backward-moving world, it may well be that leadership toward return to a new and forward-moving world is to rest with the United States. Despite our shortcomings and failures, we have written a record on the history of the last one hundred and fifty years which is not only of outstanding importance, but full of promise for the future.

We have established the oldest form of government now existing in the world and we have shown its capacity to continue to exist, unaltered in principle, through all the stupendous changes of a century and a half.

We have established in permanent form the federal principle, and it is that principle which must be applied if a new, a forward-facing, a prosperous and a peaceful world is to be built upon the wreck and the ruin of that backward-moving world at which we now look.

We have established freedom of trade among these federal units and have given to each unit fullest opportunity to develop its resources and the capacity of its population. This, again, is a principle which must be recognized and accepted in a contented and a peaceful world composed of nations, some great and some small, but all proud of their independence and of their capacity for human service.

We have established the authority of an independent judicial system, which means that not force nor the gain-seeking impulse, but right and justice, shall be accepted and enforced as ruling principles of human intercourse, whether personal, group or national. This, too, is a principle which must dominate a newly organized and a forward-moving world.

The great progress which had been made in applying these fundamental principles to world organization and world life has been, for the time being, completely stopped, but there are those of us who have faith that it will not be long before those principles will again be turned to as fundamental and controlling.

It must be remembered that the peoples held for the moment under brutal dictatorship are each and all highly civilized. They have, each and all, made literally great contributions to literature and to science, to art and to industry. Who can possibly believe that when the emotional spasm is over—and that may be earlier than we now think—they will fail to assert themselves in terms of their old ambitions and their old principles? When that time comes—and may it come soon—where can these peoples turn save to the United States, to see at work, and on the whole successfully at work, those underlying principles of government, of life and of conduct which are the outgrowth of liberty and which alone make the continuance of liberty possible? All that we need to do is to make sure, always and everywhere, that gain-seeking, whether for individuals or for groups, is subordinated to public service. Would not Washington and Hamilton, Jefferson and Madison, Webster and Lincoln and our other great national leaders of the past, looking down from their home in high heaven, let their faces shine with contentment as they saw those principles and habits of life which they did so much to establish gaining control over what has become a wrecked and a backward-moving world, in order to turn it into a new, a contented, a prosperous and a peaceful organized family of nations, worldwide in scope and safe beyond peradventure from the despot of tomorrow?

We may take encouragement from the little-remembered happenings of nearly a century and a half ago. For some twenty years Napoleon Bonaparte dominated by force the greater part of Europe and part of Africa and set his heart on the subjugation of liberty-loving Great Britain. To the statesmen of that day, the world upon which they looked seemed very much like the world by which we ourselves are confronted. It was liberalism which was struggling for its life and which was so gravely threatened that there was general despair concerning it. Hear these words spoken in the House of Commons by the younger Pitt on April 25, 1804, when Great Britain was arming itself to resist the invasion which Napoleon had planned, and see how absolutely they apply to what is now happening in the world:

I need not remind the house that we are come to a new æra in the history of nations; that we are called to struggle for the destiny, not of this country alone, but of the civilized world. We must remember that it is not for ourselves alone that we submit to unexampled privations. We have for ourselves the great duty of self-preservation to perform; but the duty of the people of England now is of a nobler and higher order. We are in the first place to provide for our security against an enemy whose malignity to this country knows no bounds: but this is not to close the views or the efforts of our exertion in so sacred a cause. Amid the wreck and the misery of nations, it is our just exultation, that we have continued superior to all that ambition or that despotism could effect, and our still higher exultation ought to be, that we provide not only for our own safety, but hold out a prospect to nations now bending under the iron yoke of tyranny, what the exertions of a free people can effect; and that at least in this corner of the world, the name of liberty is still revered, cherished, and sanctified.[4]

It was eleven years later that Waterloo brought Napoleon's despotic career to an end and paved the way for the progress which European nations have since made.

May we not hope and pray that a twentieth-century Waterloo is not far distant?

[4]Pitt, William, *Speeches . . . in the House of Commons*, second edition. London: Longman, Hurst, Rees and Orme, 1808. Vol. III, pp. 362–363.

IX

THE JOY OF WORK

An address delivered at the opening of the
187th year of Columbia University
September 25, 1940

THE JOY OF WORK

When Longfellow wrote of

> ". . . . . the joy
> That springs from labor"

he was writing for a generation which has passed. There has now grown up, certainly in the United States and to no inconsiderable extent in other lands as well, a curious antipathy to work. The fact that work is the fundamental activity of our civilization, as well as the foundation upon which that civilization rests, and not a form of oppression or of punishment, seems to be almost entirely forgotten. Everywhere there is pressure to reduce the hours of labor to a minimum and even to reduce the production in those limited hours to another minimum, neither of which has any relation to health, to fatigue or to the individual's capacity. These restrictions increase the cost of living for every one, including the workman himself. If, for example, a bricklayer may only lay 800 bricks in a working day, when it would easily be possible for him, because of skill, to lay 1000 or 1200, he is multiplying the cost of construction and thereby inevitably diminishing the demand for skilled labor, including his own.

What may be the object of these efforts to reduce labor

to a minimum is not clear, since they are not in the interest of him who works; for if one can escape from work or can find no opportunity for work, he must become a dependent upon somebody or something. This means that his own independence is lost. As a dependent, his laborless time is turned into leisure. How many human beings are capable of making good use of leisure or of understanding what the opportunities of leisure are? That understanding is one of the best products of a liberal education. Sports are well enough in their way, but, save for those who are professionally devoted to them, they cannot occupy more than a limited amount of one's free time. There are, of course, many uses of leisure which are wholly admirable, but it requires some knowledge and some experience to know how to take advantage of them.

The human world as we know it is the product of work—work with the hands or work with the brain. Its progress is made possible only by work. It is work which has lifted us out of brute life. It may be work which is tiresome, it may be work which is nerve-racking or it may be work which brings with it satisfaction and delight. In any case it must be work. Everything depends upon whether the individual human being understands his work and what it means and what part it plays in the human economy, and whether he is ready and willing to do his very best to make his work productive and helpful to his fellow men. If his only desire is to do as little work as possible and to be paid as much as possible for doing it, then his case is hopeless. He is an uncivilized being. If he is a free and moral human being, he will want to do his very best in whatever his occupation may be, and he will not wish to be limited, either in the character or the amount of his work, by the capacity for work of a neighbor who may not be so competent or so well trained as himself.

Recognition should be given to excellence of manual work similar to that given to excellence of intellectual work. On Morningside Heights, it has been our established custom, when a new academic building is completed, to hold a formal gathering of all the workmen who have been engaged upon its construction and equipment. To this gathering members of the workmen's families are also invited. In the presence of this company the President of the University awards a medal, accompanied by a certificate, to that manual workman in each of the trades engaged upon the building who has been chosen to receive it because of the excellence of his work in its construction or equipment. Those who are to receive these medals are selected by a committee consisting of a representative of the University, a representative of the architect, a representative of the contractor and a representative of the trade or type of work for excellence in which the medal is to be awarded. These gatherings have been impressive in high degree and have given to the workmen a consciousness of the fact that the University regards them as contributing directly to its equipment for usefulness in its chosen field of endeavor and for its helpfulness to mankind. This proceeding is quite analogous to that of conferring a University Medal or an honorary degree at the annual Commencement.

Every attempt, by whatever authority, to fix a maximum of productive labor by a given worker in a given time is an unjust restriction upon his freedom and a limitation of his right to make the most of himself in order that he may rise in the scale of the social and economic order in which he lives. The notion that all human beings born into this world enter at birth into a definite social and economic classification, in which classification they must remain permanently through life, is wholly false and fatal to a progressive civilization. It means the invention and installation of an artificial class system where no such thing should exist. It strikes at the very roots of the possibility to which every healthy-minded man looks: the possibility that he may, as life goes on, come by his own efforts into a larger and more important field of activity than the one in which his work began. In the United States our industrial history abounds in illustrations of the capacity of men who began their life-work at the very bottom of the industrial or administrative scale to rise to posts of highest authority and responsibility by their own efforts and their own excellence.

The false doctrine of permanent social and economic classes contradicts and undermines the whole structure of democracy and lays the foundation for the quick building of a class struggle, perhaps even a class war, which, if carried on long enough and severely enough, would bring democracy to an end. It is one of despotism's ways of beginning its career.

Each one of us should be able to repeat with conviction and enthusiasm these words of Amiel:

"What I want is work. It is work which gives flavor to life.

Mere existence without object and without effort is a poor thing."[1]

This is what is meant by the joy of work. To another year of joyous work I am happy to welcome this company of scholars and their students.

[1]Amiel's *Journal*. Translated by Mrs. Humphry Ward. (New York: Macmillan Company, 1894.) Vol. II, p. 348.

X

GOOD NEIGHBORS

An address delivered at the dinner
in honor of the recipients of the Cabot Prizes in Journalism
Waldorf-Astoria Hotel
November 6, 1940

[Broadcast to Latin America by the National Broadcasting
Company. Recorded by means of phonograph.]

GOOD NEIGHBORS

Believe me, this is a most significant occasion. It means more at this hour in the world's history than would be possible at any other time which has preceded it. It is an evidence of our determination as Americans to turn the Good Neighbor policy from a declaration of words into deeds and policies of understanding and co-operation. We have arrived at a point where the responsibility of the Americas is far greater than it has ever been and where the demands upon their capacity, their ideals and their high intelligence will be literally enormous. It is only about two hundred years since Bishop Berkeley wrote the oft-quoted words, "Westward the course of empire takes its way," and now we see the course of empire taking its way westward because of conditions and happenings which no one would have ventured even a generation ago to predict as possible.

One of my most moving memories is to have stood on the spot where Christopher Columbus landed when he reached this continent, and then to have been taken by the Archbishop of Santo Domingo to stand in the presence of Columbus' remains. An American of any imagination and any historic sense could not but be deeply moved by those experiences. From that day to this it has been my habit to think more and more of the significance of what Columbus did and of the long time it has taken us to see the possibilities which lie before us and to enter upon the task of their accomplishment. We have dwelt, wisely enough, upon economic relationships and upon the economic interdependence of the American peoples. But that economic interdependence will move with twice its rapidity if it rests upon a basis of intellectual interdependence and understanding. If our great organs of opinion, if the leaders and exponents of the intellectual life—in letters, in science, in law, in medicine, in engineering, in theology—if they come to understand each other and to know of each other's doings day by day, the world will be a different place. They will then surely be determined each to strengthen the hands of the other in making America, as a half of the whole world, bear its full share of responsibility, not only for protecting the great achievements of Western Civilization, but for strengthening them, developing them and carrying them forward. We can, and must, show to peoples older than ourselves who have now fallen victims to a reactionary radicalism the like of which the world has never seen, what they might still achieve were they to turn their eyes westward. There they would see the fundamental principles of the Bill of Rights of the Federal Constitution accepted as the basic document of the public life of every American people, defended, illustrated and practised by them, each and all, to the end that liberty may not perish from this earth.

If we are to accomplish any such undertaking even in modest degree, the very first agency of which we wish to make use is that of journalism. What we need is not only the gathering, the printing and the circulation of the news day by day, but also its judicious and fair

interpretation by correspondents and editorial writers
of the highest ability and insight. We need the co-
operation of our universities on both continents. We
need the co-operation of our men of letters in every
land. We need the co-operation of our men of science
wherever they may be at work. We need a larger understanding of our three languages—English, Spanish and
Portuguese. In addition to all that, we need the conviction that we are pursuing in all these things a high intellectual and moral end, which has almost infinite
meaning for the civilization of this world.

Any one who will take pains to go back over the great
periods in the development of Western Civilization
will see that at intervals, long intervals—hundreds,
sometimes thousands of years—all that had been accomplished, collapsed. Imagine what the great buildings in upper Egypt must have looked like before they
were destroyed and covered with the sands of the desert!
Imagine what Nineveh and Babylon must have looked
like, with their buildings designed precisely as the Empire State Building of today is designed, having a
height of two hundred, three hundred, four hundred
feet, standing in the midst of a great community given
over to the ideals and habits of the life of that period.
The men of that time thought that they had come
permanently into control of the world's civilization!
Yet today we are digging them out from the sands that
have covered them for centuries, and are astounded at
what we find there of the evidence of what those peoples
had done.

Civilization can be destroyed. Its physical evidences
can be made invisible. Its intellectual achievements can

be forgotten—all these only to be exhumed in part after many generations. They are then studied and interpreted by the scholars of what was once a distant tomorrow. Can it be that the world is heading for another collapse like that?

If so, the Americas must busy themselves quickly and with complete understanding to do their part in holding up those ideals and principles, and practising them, which will assure us of the continuance of all that is best in Western Civilization. We must strengthen those principles and apply them to the needs and the hopes of man. It is upon these considerations that I wish to put the greatest stress before this gathering tonight.

XI

RELIGION AND FAITH IN EDUCATION

An address delivered at Columbia University
on the occasion of the rededication of Earl Hall
November 28, 1940

RELIGION AND FAITH IN EDUCATION

At this hour in the history of the world this simple and dignified ceremonial is full of encouragement. Here we are facing the future in terms of the best which the past has to offer. We are doing it in the broadest possible spirit of human sympathy and human understanding, and we are doing it in terms of faith which is adjoined to knowledge.

When Earl Hall was given to Columbia forty years ago, it was given in terms which I like to call catholic, using that word without a capital. Mr. Dodge, himself a devout and devoted member of the Presbyterian Church, provided in his deed of gift for the use of this building by organizations of Roman Catholic students or of Hebrew students as well as of Protestant students. They were all invited on equal terms to friendly and generous co-operation toward one and the same high religious aim.

In this day and generation we are beginning to forget the place which religious instruction must occupy in education if that education is to be truly sound and liberal. We seem to forget that until some two hundred years ago religious instruction everywhere dominated education; religion guided education, shaped education and selected the material for education in every part of the world—in the Orient, in Europe and in the Americas. Then began, as a result of the rise of Protestantism and the spread of democracy, those sharp differences of religious opinion and of religious worship which unfortunately exhibited themselves in highly controversial form. One consequence was to lead men to turn aside from religious study and religious teaching in the attempt to avoid those unfortunate contentious differences which had become so common. Then, particularly in this democracy of ours, a curious tendency grew up to exclude religious teaching altogether from education on the ground that such teaching was in conflict with our fundamental doctrine as to the separation of church and state. In other words, religious teaching was narrowed down to something which might be called denominationalism, and therefore because of differences of faith and practice it must be excluded from education. The result was to give paganism new importance and new influence.

In my own school days the morning exercises in the public schools of my home town in New Jersey opened with the Lord's Prayer repeated by the entire company of pupils and followed by the reading of a chapter of the Bible. There was then sung a hymn from the school hymn book, after which the children went to their several classrooms. That was brought to an end by the decision of the Supreme Court of the state of Wisconsin written in 1890, holding that this practice was unconstitutional because it permitted an intermingling of church and state in public schools supported by taxation. In handing down that opinion the Court took pains to emphasize the importance of religious instruction and pointed out that it was the duty of the family and the church to give it. It is because the family and the church have not risen to their responsibilities during this past half-century, that religious instruction has so largely passed out of education and that religious knowledge is so largely lacking among the youth of yesterday and today.

It must be remembered that, after all is said and done, our country is a religious country. Every day when the Senate of the United States meets, every day when the House of Representatives convenes, the business of the day is opened with a prayer offered by the Chaplain, in the one case of the Senate and in the other case of the House of Representatives. This Chaplain is a Christian minister. The same is true of both houses of the Legislature of the State of New York and of many other state legislatures. In other words, separation of church and state does not mean that we are a pagan people. It simply means that being a religious and a Christian people as well, we must also be catholic, again using that word with a small "c."

The Legislature of the State of New York has only just now passed a statute restoring the American system in the state of New York by providing that at a certain time each week all pupils in a public school shall be set free to receive such religious instruction as their parents may prefer from teachers of that form of religious faith which their parents choose. This statute realizes that the United States is not pagan but that it is a religious people and must have freedom of religious teaching and of religious faith. This particular system was first introduced in France when, after the political and social revolution which followed the war of 1870–71, the French Parliament in 1882 overturned the school system as then organized. In its new legislation it provided that the public-school pupils should be set free on each Thursday and allowed to go to the church or religious institution of the teacher which their parents might select, for religious instruction. Of course, if their parents preferred paganism, that day would be for their children a holiday; otherwise, the children would receive religious instruction in the form which their parents desired.

It is just a little more than forty years ago that I presented my views on this subject before the Sunday School Commission of the Diocese of New York, my subject being "Religious Instruction and Its Relation to Education." For the first time in years, I looked over that address today, it being printed in my volume, *The Meaning of Education.*[1] I do not find one single word in the argument which I then advanced that I would change today. Conditions as they then presented themselves have become even more serious, and the solution of the problem which I offered at that time is to me even more obvious today than it was then. The fundamental thing to remember is that education is the joint product of the influence of the family, the church and the school. The school has but a very limited and a very definite function to perform. The family and the church have very considerable functions to perform which, unhappily, they are increasingly neglecting. Until the family and the church can be roused to the full height of their responsibility we cannot expect to find the youth of the land in possession of that religious

[1]Nicholas Murray Butler, *The Meaning of Education*, revised edition (New York: Charles Scribner's Sons, 1915), pp. 179–200.

knowledge and religious feeling which were characteristic of their ancestors two or three generations ago.

There is also a very curious lack in our course of
college study, of which I have spoken during past years.
I have never known a course of instruction to be offered
to undergraduates on the "Influence of Faith in Shaping Western Civilization." All our instruction is based
on the influence of knowledge—literature, science, the
arts, politics. As a matter of fact, knowledge as opposed
to faith had practically no influence in shaping Western
civilization until four or five hundred years ago. For
some three thousand years civilization was shaped by
faith in one of its many forms—Hindu, Brahmin, Hebrew, Christian or Mohammedan. It was that faith
which guided men in their ambitions and in their social
and political policies. It is only three or four hundred
years since knowledge began to displace faith as a controlling influence, and we are mistaken when we look
at past history if we put the emphasis upon knowledge
from the beginning of recorded time. This would be a
very inspiring course of instruction were it to be given
by some scholar well schooled in the history of religious
faith, familiar with the various religions and with some
insight into the personalities which were guiding forces
from century to century in Europe's civilization. The
youth of tomorrow would then begin to realize that the
foundations of all that we are now doing were not originally laid by knowledge at all, but by some form of
that faith to which all knowledge was subordinate until
the beginning of the intellectual revolution which co-
incided with the beginning of our modern scientific era.

In respect to all this the history of our religious life

and work at Columbia shows it to have been of the most admirable and satisfactory sort. When the first charter of King's College was granted in 1754, among the Board of Governors were the Archbishop of Canterbury, the rector of Trinity Church, the senior minister of the Reformed Protestant Dutch Church (the oldest in Manhattan), the minister of the ancient Lutheran Church, the minister of the French Church and the minister of the Presbyterian Congregation, these being all the churches that were then on Manhattan Island. That charter provided, at a time when religious tension and religious feeling ran very high, that the Trustees of this newly founded college should never be empowered to make any discrimination against teacher or student on account of his religious faith or his religious relationship. So far as I know, this and the very similar provision which was put into the first charter of the College of New Jersey—now Princeton University—founded eight years earlier than King's College, now Columbia University, are the first charter provisions of their kind. Columbia has remained true to that tradition. So it welcomes and has welcomed students and teachers of every form of religious faith when they are honest, sincere, high-minded, genuine. We wish to avoid these unnecessary and bitter theological controversies. We look not only with dismay, but with more than that, upon the violent anti-Semitic movements which find expression from time to time among the American people and which now have been taken up in so cruel a form by despotic governments in various parts of the world. We look with dismay at those passionate expressions of ignorance which are called the Ku Klux Klan and their attack upon members and priests of the Roman Catholic Church. Both anti-Semitism and the Ku Klux Klan are an insult to democracy and a contradiction of it.

But faith—honest, sincere, hopeful—opens a door to moving forward in this new and very difficult world in which our children must live. It opens the door into that world in a spirit inspired by something more than the merely human, the gain-seeking and the temporary. It brings us, our children and our grandchildren, in touch with the eternal verities which are the only possible foundation for a civilization and a life that are worthy of human ambition and human endeavor.

XII

WHAT WAY OUT?

NEW YEAR'S MESSAGE, 1941

A statement written for the press
on New Year's Day, 1941

WHAT WAY OUT?

NEW YEAR'S MESSAGE, 1941

What will the new year bring? Must we look forward to a continuance of the control by cruel force of a large part of what we still like to call the civilized world? Must the slaughter on a gigantic scale of innocent and non-combatant men, women and children continue unchecked? Must the destruction of the world's power of economic production, as well as of its accumulated savings for generations, go on indefinitely, to the impoverishment of mankind? Is it possible that no way can be found by the tens of millions of human beings who detest war and who are eagerly desirous of permanent peace, to break the control over them by those small minorities which, chiefly by the use of influences which are psychological in origin and in method, have led or thrown them into a self-destructive war which they abhor in principle and which antagonizes their own highest interests?

What cause can be given for the gigantic collapse of the rule of intelligence, of morals and of law, on which we look as this new year opens? What has happened to the great democracies of the world, which have been some two centuries in building and which were thought to be established on so sound a basis that nothing could weaken or overturn them? Have they failed to give this modern world that leadership which it had to have if it was to move forward on a high plane of liberal and increasingly competent democracy? What has happened to those other highly civilized nations not yet democratic in form or in temper but in which the spirit of democracy was steadily growing?

We Americans must try to answer these questions and learn to look facts in the face, particularly as these facts relate to our own share of responsibility for what is happening. It is no European war on which we look, but a world-wide war in which every nation is engaged and from which every nation will suffer severely. The military contest, in which not all nations are taking part, is only one—and of course the most appalling—manifestation of this world war. It is the economic, the social, the political and the intellectual conflict which is universal and world-wide, and which has brought about the military conflict. This military conflict may itself grow to like world-wide dimensions unless it collapses or can be checked in the not distant future.

It is the plain teaching of history that there is only one way to avoid war, and that is first to limit and then in time to remove the causes of war. This requires world-wide international co-operation. Every upholder of a policy of national isolation, no matter what he may profess, is really at work to make war possible and to injure the interests of his own people. His policies would even greatly increase the chance that his government might have to participate in the military contest of any war, with every probability of facing defeat through lack of understanding and of preparation.

How different this world of 1941 would have been

had American public policy followed the leadership of those men of foresight and vision who began to point the way toward permanent peace a long generation ago! Their ideals and program of action received the formal endorsement and support of both great American political parties in the declarations of policy and of promise adopted by their national conventions of 1920 and explicitly accepted by their candidates for the presidency in that year. Suppose that the Republican Party had realized the full significance of the great declaration made by President McKinley at Buffalo, New York, on September 5, 1901, the day before he fell by the hand of an assassin:

The period of exclusiveness is past. The expansion of our trade and commerce is the pressing problem. Commercial wars are unprofitable. A policy of good will and friendly trade relations will prevent reprisals. Reciprocity treaties are in harmony with the spirit of the times, measures of retaliation are not.

Unhappily, McKinley's tragic death prevented the echo of those noble words from being heard by the American people. There next came the notable and forward-facing speech on international peace delivered by Theodore Roosevelt before the Nobel Prize Committee at Christiania in Norway on May 5, 1910. He then offered a definite plan to promote world organization and world peace by international arbitration, by the development of The Hague Tribunal and by an international agreement to check armaments, especially naval armaments, and to form a league of peace, not only to keep the peace among the members of the league, but to prevent, by force if necessary, its being broken by others. Then came the extraordinary resolution passed in June, 1910, by both houses of the American Congress, without a single dissenting vote in either house and signed by President Taft, providing for the appointment of a commission of five members by the President of the United States to consider the expediency of utilizing existing international agencies for the purpose of limiting the armaments of the nations of the world by international agreement and of constituting the combined navies of the world an international force for the preservation of universal peace. Here was a truly American program of progress, agreed upon by unanimous consent. Here were three Presidents—McKinley, Theodore Roosevelt and Taft—joined later by Presidents Wilson and Harding and the entire membership of both houses of the American Congress, in open and emphatic opposition to that doctrine of isolation which we are so constantly told is to be accepted as traditional American policy. It is not and never has been traditional American policy. The change of very few votes in the Senate would have accepted the Treaty of Versailles with the reservations which were proposed in 1919–20. That acceptance would of itself have given to the American people leadership in the reconstitution of the world of a generation ago through policies which might well have led the way to national and international prosperity and peace. Similarly, the change of but very few votes in the Senate on January 29, 1935, would have affirmed our concurrence in the establishment of the international court to put in practice the great principle of the judicial settlement of international disputes, which our own statesmen had offered to the world and which the rest of the world was ready to accept.

We may find fault with the other democracies. We may see much to criticize in the policies followed by the governments of France and of Great Britain during the past generation. We may be severe and emphatic in our criticism of the peoples of Germany and of Italy who have permitted their governments to appeal to force in the field of international policy; but we must first of all look ourselves in the face. What have we been doing since McKinley's speech at Buffalo to follow in the field of public policy the high ideals which our leaders have offered to us and to which both great political parties had pledged themselves? If we say that it is distressing that the peoples of Germany and of Italy cannot control their governments sufficiently to hold them back from military war, may not those people turn to us and ask, why is it that the American people could not make their government follow the declarations of their chosen leaders? Why could they not make their elected representatives at Washington keep their pledges to the people? Perhaps it will be well to press these questions pretty vigorously in this year of 1941, if the year 1942 and those to come after it are to have any measure of happiness for us. The path of progress has been pointed out to us and we have been formally pledged to follow it—why do we not do so?

Is not this the time to invite our fellow Americans and their governments, from Canada on the north to Argentina and Chile on the south, to join us in a movement to defend democracy by giving all possible aid short of engaging in military war to those peoples which are fighting its battle, in the hope that we may speedily bring the present chaos to an end and begin to lay the firm foundations for an organized, a peaceful and a prosperous world? This cannot be done in an instant, but surely there is no time to be lost in entering upon the task.

If it be said that any such effort at this time is wholly impracticable, then what is the alternative? Must the world face chaos and the overturn of its liberal and democratic civilization, as well as the destruction of the foundation upon which that civilization rests, because it lacks the courage—or it may be the temerity—to attempt to save the stupendous human gains of the past five hundred years? Nothing is impracticable which the world's intelligence, the world's courage and the world's idealism are united to undertake.

XIII

LIBERALISM IN THIS TIRED WORLD

An address delivered at the Annual Meeting
of the Pilgrims of the United States
Hotel Biltmore, New York
January 22, 1941

LIBERALISM IN THIS TIRED WORLD

We are living in a tired world. It is also a disappointed world. The truly great movement of constructive and forward-facing liberal opinion which began to manifest itself with great power some four centuries ago, has become weak and exhausted. The record which that movement made in writing modern history and in shaping the thought and the institutions of men is without parallel.

It brought about, first, the English revolution of the seventeenth century, and then, in part through the effect of that revolution which reached France through Voltaire's famous *Lettres sur les Anglais*, it brought about, in concurrence with other forces, the great French Revolution of the close of the eighteenth century. Meanwhile, it had brought into existence on this side of the Atlantic, the Federal Union of thirteen states and had written the famous Bill of Rights into the Federal Constitution of those United States, marking its supreme achievement. There is no like record of accomplishment for any force or ideals since the beginning of history.

Then came, for a quarter century, the powerful reaction led by Napoleon Bonaparte; and it seemed for a time as if that liberal movement had come to its end. But there was a Waterloo. After Waterloo, liberal, constructive political, social and economic philosophy resumed its march. It became particularly powerful in England and in France and in the smaller European countries.

What truly great names are those which are associated with that movement from the middle of the eighteenth century on toward the close of the nineteenth! In England, there are the names of Chatham and of Burke, of Fox and of Pitt, of Palmerston and of Cobden, of Bright and of Gladstone. In France, there are those of Chateaubriand and of Lamartine, of Thiers and of Gambetta; and in Italy the names of Mazzini and of Cavour. On our side of the Atlantic, we write on the high places of history the names of Washington and of Franklin, of Hamilton and of Jefferson, of Madison and of Clay, of Webster and of Lincoln. Where else, in all the history of mankind, can be found a group of names like these, names of men who, in England, in France, in Italy and in the United States, transplanted liberalism to a new soil, put its roots down deep, and had it bear rich fruit in the thought and the institutions of mankind?

And then came the evidences of fatigue. They began ·to manifest themselves at the turn of the last century, when this great development, three hundred and fifty years old, found itself confronted by an entirely new series of facts and forces which were the result of the industrial revolution, now more than a hundred years old, and of the stupendous achievements in the field of science and invention, which had so completely altered the facts of daily life and of every industry, of commerce and of finance.

Confronted by that stupendous series of problems,

constructive liberalism began to falter and to halt. Men began to turn backward and to ask whether perhaps we had not gone too far in establishing and defending human liberty, in making possible freedom of speech, freedom of the press, freedom of thought, freedom of work, freedom of religion, and whether there should not be a closer and more highly centralized organization of all human effort.

There had been individuals preaching this reactionary doctrine for the better part of a hundred years, but they were not listened to in any great degree until these new industrial, social and economic problems began to face the whole world with such force and in such number that men hesitated to act in terms of what had been for generations their fundamental underlying convictions.

And there is where the world is today. It is tired by that stupendous effort. It is disappointed that the great movement of progress has been checked. It has been checked because the liberal philosophy, sound as it is, had not yet obtained a sufficient hold over the minds of great masses of men, despite the teachings of leaders of opinion and of the intellectual life, to enable them to approach these new problems in its spirit. Therefore they were ready to hesitate instead of to act. It is one more illustration of the truth of the maxim that "he who hesitates is lost."

Our liberal philosophy has hesitated. It has undertaken to question some of its own fundamental principles and it has opened the door to the greatest reactionary force the world knows, which is armed force. The moment that liberalism halts, sooner or later men in so-called free countries under free forms of government will always find themselves confronted by reactionary radicalism. It is characteristic of reactionary radicalism that it calls itself liberal. It is in truth the very contradiction of everything for which liberalism stands. It is radical because it wishes to pull up by the roots whatever exists. It is reactionary because it wishes to go back and begin all over again that advance of mankind which for four thousand years has been developing toward this liberal social order which came to such a climax and bore such fruit in the period through which civilization has just now passed.

What has been the aim of liberalism? The aim of liberalism has been to make it plain that the individual is not to be subject to the compulsion of the group, but that the group is organized in a political or economic state for a common purpose which will leave the individual free in his thought, in his speech, in his religion, and in his press. This radical movement is an attempt to substitute compulsion for freedom. It is an attempt to substitute a common possession of all the world's product instead of encouraging the individual himself to do his best in a spirit, not of gain-seeking only, but of human service. And there is the fundamental conflict in every form of human life. It is gain-seeking versus human service. Unless gain-seeking be subordinated to human service, no social or economic society can survive or ought to survive.

If the individual is set free, it is with the expectation and the hope that his controlling motive will be ultimately human service. He will then do his best. He will earn, he will save, he will contribute; but the earning and the savings will be incidental and secondary to a spirit of helping and guiding his fellow men. That conception of a liberal society is what marked and characterized the great historic liberal movement of which I speak. That which has made that movement grow tired is the failure of that motive of human service to hold its own in the face of new and desperately difficult problems which, I repeat, the industrial revolution and the epoch-marking advances in science and invention have brought to mankind.

When we examine these well-known historic facts, we are confronted by the question of what our own present attitude should be. To that question, I give but one answer. It must never be surrender! It must never be apathy. It must never be cowardice. It must never be a perpetual state of intellectual, moral, economic and political fatigue. We must and shall resume that march, repel and hold back this new instrument of brute force, so cruelly exercised, and go behind it to the very people in whose name it is now used and who themselves are being desperately oppressed by it. We must go back to a conception of an orderly and liberal being and friendly society toward which we had made so great progress when the twentieth century opened.

That requires courage. That requires capacity for work in a spirit of unselfish human service. That requires insight. If this world is ever going to have perpetual peace, we must have, first, a community of principle which leads to a community of action, and which in turn ultimately leads to a community of interest. We can make conflicting interests cease to conflict only if we can get below the surface of things and show men in what their community of interest consists, be it individual or group or national or international.

It will not do for the English-speaking peoples to weaken in their leadership of the liberal movement in politics, in the social and economic order and in the intellectual life. They are committed to that movement by their achievement and by their great leaders of the mind. The greater part of their history is a glorious tribute to its success and its distinction.

No, for the Pilgrims and those for whom they speak —our fellow men in the British Commonwealth of Nations, in old Greece with its glorious achievement of today, or in any other part of the world where these fundamental principles are accepted, defended and illustrated—there is our opportunity for leadership and for co-operation!

Let me quote, as a suitable motto for the Pilgrims at this crisis, the very remarkable paragraph with which the President of the United States ended his third inaugural address:

We do not retreat. We are not content to stand still. As Americans, we go forward in the service of our country, by the will of God!

I give that as a motto for the Pilgrims of today and tomorrow.

XIV

DEMOCRACY REQUIRES ACTION

Extract from Annual Report for 1940 of the
Director of the
Division of Intercourse and Education
Carnegie Endowment for International Peace
March 1, 1941

DEMOCRACY REQUIRES ACTION

The year 1940 has set the low water-mark in the history of Western civilization. The total collapse of intellectual honesty, of respect for the rights of the weak and unoffending, of moral principle and of law, both national and international, has passed the limits of the conceivable. The world has returned for the time being to the rule of cruel and relentless brute force, the declared object of which is the establishment of a so-called New Order. What that order may be passes human comprehension. It certainly cannot be anything even remotely related to the institutions of that liberal, broad-minded and progressive civilization which has been for centuries in the making. The Nazis describe this New Order as Lebensraum. To the rest of the world it is Todesraum.

Most appalling is the breakdown of the once great German people. After centuries of steady and orderly development, that people in the eighteenth and nineteenth centuries reached a height where they were guiding and enriching the thought of the world. In philosophy, in literature, in music, in the fine arts and in orderly industrial development they were setting the standard for a world in which their influence was commanding. From that great height they have fallen almost overnight to their present low level of merely animal existence. Who would have thought a people which hailed *Zum ewigen Frieden,* the classic work of Immanuel Kant, greatest of German philosophers, could have become a victim of the emotional, irrational and almost brutal doctrines of Adolf Hitler's *Mein Kampf?* Yet just that has happened. At the moment, the world-wide struggle between this violent reaction and the forward-facing philosophy of a truly modern and progressive civilization hangs in the balance. Are the Goths, the Huns and the Vandals once again to tear down the structure of civilization and set the Western World back for a thousand years or will civilization in that Western World be able so to exert its powers and so to defend its ideals as to drive these new barbarians back to the primeval forest out of which they came?

Unfortunately, the democracies have been very slow and unready to recognize the significance and the character of the attack being made upon those fundamental principles which are their foundation. Now, however, they are coming to recognize that this new invasion is directed at all of them, wherever they may be, whether in Europe, in Asia or in the Americas. The object of the so-called New Order is specifically declared to be to displace that social, economic and political liberty which has been so widely established during the past three hundred years and so highly acclaimed by the leaders of the world's thought.

In the midst of so amazing and so terrifying a conflict, it must be the object of the Carnegie Endowment for International Peace to direct attention to the real significance of this conflict, to appeal to the democracies to show power of leadership and constructive policy and so to act in effective co-operation that they will not only protect but in the end strengthen all those principles and ideals for which they stand and which are essential to their life.

From the point of view of an American, it can only once more be repeated that to speak of this war as a European war is childish. To describe it as something from which the American government and the American people may and should remain aloof and isolated is worse than stupidity. It is suicidal.

The Carnegie Endowment must also direct its attention, as we have so often insisted, upon the postwar reconstruction of this world in terms of a social, an economic and a political organization and of co-operation between nations which will show that the lessons of this fearful contest have really been learned. Democracy does not mean perpetual discussion and debate. It also means action. If democracy does nothing but debate, then the Goths, the Huns and the Vandals will take care that something really happens when it will be too late for the democracies successfully to resist. Democracy must choose its leaders, men responsible to it but given for the time being that full power and official responsibility which is needed for leadership in such a crisis as now exists. Unless these fundamental principles and facts can be grasped and acted upon, the democracies will find the door closed not only to their advance but even to their continued existence.

Once more it is important to strike the note of hopefulness and courage. We must not yield to the temptation to assume that all is lost, but must strengthen our minds and our bodies to continue the great contest between civilization and barbarism until victory for civilization be finally and definitely gained.

XV

THE THREAT OF THE NEW ORDER

An address delivered at the dinner given
by the Pilgrims of the United States
in honor of the Viscount Halifax,
The Waldorf-Astoria, New York
March 25, 1941

THE THREAT OF THE NEW ORDER

Tonight we offer the heartiest of welcomes to the distinguished statesman who has come to us as British Ambassador at Washington. He has crossed the war-tossed Atlantic Ocean under conditions of great danger in order that he may represent the British Government and the British people to the American Government and the American people as British Ambassador at Washington. That is a great and influential and honorable post at any time, but today it is one of the most important posts in the public life of the whole world. It is a lighthouse which makes plain how the public opinion of Great Britain may best reach the public opinion of the United States, and how the public opinion of the United States may best reach Great Britain to the end that these two great branches of the English-speaking peoples may be in fullest understanding and co-operation at this critical moment in the world's history.

We are face to face with what Lord Gorell has just now described as the dreariest, deadliest war that has ever disgraced the annals of mankind. We are face to face with a carefully organized and violently executed attack upon the fundamental principles of that form of civilization in which we believe and on that form of life and government which we call freedom, liberty or democracy.

There is no concealment of purpose on the part of those who are undertaking this attack. They tell us frankly that they have in mind a New Order, something which they do not define or describe, beyond telling us that it makes democracy and liberty absolutely impossible. That is why the English-speaking peoples have come to understand the character of the attack being made upon them and why it is that American public opinion is giving to the British people who are carrying on this defense in most magnificent and courageous fashion, every aid which is in its power.

It is two long generations since Abraham Lincoln said to the American people that their government could not exist half slave and half free. If Abraham Lincoln were on this earth tonight, he would say the same thing about this twentieth-century world. It cannot exist half slave and half free.

The institutions which, going way back to Magna Carta and coming down through the long stretch of British history, found their climax in the Bill of Rights of the Federal Constitution of the United States, are those which are under attack at this moment. It is not England primarily, it is not the United States, it is not Canada, and it is not Latin-America; it is any people which supports those principles and endeavors to build its civilization upon them which this New Order is trying to overturn. That attack is not necessarily of a military character. It may be in a hundred other ways with which we have now become familiar. Ask Denmark, ask Norway, ask the Netherlands, ask Belgium, ask Roumania, ask Bulgaria, and ask Czechoslovakia as to what methods there may be to undermine and overturn an independent government.

At this moment we are looking out upon Great Britain and upon the descendants of the ancient Greeks as standing to the very end of their power to support the institutions which are defined in British constitutional history and in our own Bill of Rights. What could be more appalling than to look out upon France, free France, and see struck from the political records of that people the great formula, "Liberté Egalité Fraternité" which came down from the revolution of one hundred and fifty years ago? What could be more sad than to see that formula being erased from the buildings on which it was engraved as a lasting motto of French political philosophy? Liberté Egalité Fraternité have for the time being disappeared.

Are we Americans to face that kind of situation? Not if the British people can win this contest, and not if we can give them all aid in our power in order to carry on the defense of those fundamental principles which are ours.

Let us be under no illusion. It is ideas which are attacked; it is principles which are assailed; it is forms of government which are to be undermined; and this New Order, undefined and undescribed, of which we hear so much, is the enemy of every free people in the world. Now since American public opinion has grasped that fact, we are getting on in our strengthening the British and the Greeks in their military defense of all which is most dear to us.

Let there be no mistake. We are under attack in the

field of principle, in the field of political organization, in the field of economic freedom, and we are depending at the moment upon those nations which are on the firing line to conduct and carry forward our defense.

Our own future is something of which we may be confident and, I hope, proud. It is some seventy-five years ago since Disraeli made his famous statement that the American democracy was founded on principles which might some day enable it not only to organize and develop the two Americas, but to shape the future of Europe as well. That perhaps may lie in the future, but whether it does or not, it is an indication on the part of a far-seeing statesman that the American people have a part to play in a modern and a peaceful world.

For us it should be a matter of pride and satisfaction that at this crisis in the world's history, we have a President of the United States and a Prime Minister of the Government of Great Britain, who see eye to eye as they look out upon the world which faces them. They are under no illusions as to what is at stake. They are under no illusions as to what is going on. Therefore it is that tonight we salute with unusual enthusiasm and affection our distinguished guest of honor.

He comes to us after more than a quarter century of almost unexampled public service to his government and his people. He has touched almost every public interest in the English Government—agriculture, education, the Colonies, the army, the Privy Council, Governor-General of India, and finally the great Foreign Office at a time of crisis in the history of Great Britain and of the world. With this long career of distinguished service and with an intellectual history marked by his

Chancellorship of Oxford University, and with a devout insight into religious faith and religious feeling, he comes with this splendid, widely experienced, and well-rounded nature to be British Ambassador at Washington.

Let me add simply the message which the President of the United States sent a few weeks ago to the Prime Minister of Great Britain. He wrote in his own hand these verses of Longfellow:

> "Sail on, O Ship of State!
> Sail on, O Union, strong and great!
> Humanity with all its fears,
> With all the hopes of future years,
> Is hanging breathless on thy fate!"

And the Prime Minister responded with characteristic directness: "Give us the tools and we will finish the job!"

God bless them both!

XVI

THE WORLD AWAITS ANOTHER WATERLOO

An address delivered at the 187th Commencement
of Columbia University
June 3, 1941

THE WORLD AWAITS ANOTHER
WATERLOO

History makes plain the fact that as the human race developed from its elementary barbarism to a complex and many-sided civilization, there has always been one fundamental and unending conflict. That conflict is between the moral ideal of unselfish service to one's fellow men and the controlling desire for gain at whatever cost to others.

Ever since the curtain rose on the recorded happenings which constitute history, this conflict has been plainly in evidence. It is a conflict not only within the nature and personality of an individual human being, but a conflict also between groups and organized special interests, whether political or economic. Reflection upon the happenings of some five thousand years and an understanding of their true significance make it increasingly clear that the whole of human history is to be written in terms of this unending struggle. Perhaps that struggle would have been much less violent had men listened to the wise words of the 1st Viscount of Halifax, spoken some three hundred years ago: "If men considered how many things there are that riches cannot buy, they would not be so fond of them."

Time and time again, not only in the history of a few human lives, but in the history of the lives of many millions of men, victory has been won by the moral ideal. But this is not enough. The gain-seeking instinct has control of so vast a proportion of humankind that it has repeatedly reduced the moral ideal to absolute impotence. What is true of individual lives in this respect is equally true, and even more conspicuous, in the history of the building and development of those organized human units which we call nations. There have been times—not a few of them—when, to all appearance, the moral ideal was gaining ground in the formulation and execution of national policy, and when men of vision and of courage have had reason to believe that the time was approaching when that moral ideal would be sufficiently controlling to serve as the foundation for a world of co-operating nations ready to work together for prosperity and peace. Such an era appeared to be in course of development, though with interruptions and setbacks, during the latter half of the nineteenth century. There were wars—serious and damaging wars—but at the same time there was a growing consciousness of their futility and their wickedness and an increasing belief in the possibility of a world organized for peace. It was this conviction which, as the nineteenth century was about to end, led to the enthusiastic reception which was given throughout the world to the famous rescript of the Czar of all the Russias, made public on August 24, 1898. Everywhere—in Europe, in Asia, in Africa and in the Americas—there was spontaneous and enthusiastic response. The action which governments were willing to take was, however, unhappily far behind the wish of public opinion, and as formal consideration of this rescript proceeded men of light and leading began to lose

hope and courage. They felt that somehow and some-
where there were powerful forces at work to restore the
gain-seeking instinct to a place of dominance and to
make impossible any real progress toward an established
system of international peace.

Here in the United States there was genuine vision,
and one great leader after another—William McKinley,
Theodore Roosevelt, William Howard Taft, Elihu
Root and Woodrow Wilson—sounded the note of hope
and of progress toward a strengthening of the moral
ideal in international relations. Indeed, in the month
of June, 1910, the Congress of the United States by
unanimous vote of both Senate and House of Representatives called upon the President to offer the leadership of the American people and their government in
accomplishing the rule of moral principle over mere
gain-seeking in order that international peace might
finally be established among men. What happened,
through no heed having been paid to this appeal, is so
tragic and of such appalling magnitude that it need not
be recounted here.

For the time being, the moral ideal has disappeared
in all that has to do with international relations. The
gain-seeking impulse supported by brute force has taken
its place, and so far as the surface of things is concerned human civilization has gone back a full thousand
years. Inconceivable though it be, we are brought face
to face in this twentieth century with governments of
peoples once great and highly civilized, whose word
now means absolutely nothing. A pledge is something
not to be kept, but to be broken. Cruelty and national
lust have displaced human feeling and friendly inter-

national co-operation. Human life has no value, and the savings of generations are wasted month by month and almost day by day in mad attempts to dominate the whole world in pursuit of gain.

How has all this been possible? What has happened to the teachings and inspiring leadership of the great prophets and apostles of the mind, who for nearly three thousand years have been holding before mankind a vision of the moral ideal supported by intellectual power? What has become of the influence and guidance of the great religions—Christian, Moslem, Hebrew, Buddhist—with their counsels of peace and good-will, or of those of Plato and of Aristotle, of St. Augustine and of St. Thomas Aquinas, and of the outstanding captains of the mind—Spanish, Italian, French, English, German—who have for hundreds of years occupied the highest place in the citadel of human fame? The answer to these questions is not easy. Indeed, it sometimes seems impossible.

Are we, then, of this twentieth century and of this still free and independent land to lose heart and to yield to the despair which is becoming so widespread in countries other than ours? Not for one moment will we yield our faith or our courage! We may well repeat once more the words of Abraham Lincoln: "Most governments have been based on the denial of the equal rights of men; ours began by affirming those rights. We made the experiment, and the fruit is before us. Look at it—think of it!" However dark the skies may seem now, however violent and apparently irresistible are the savage attacks being made with barbarous brutality upon innocent women and children and non-combatant men, upon hospitals and institutions for the care of the aged and dependent, upon cathedrals and churches, upon libraries and galleries of the world's art, upon classic monuments which record the architectural achievements of centuries —we must not despair. Our spirit of faith in the ultimate rule of the moral ideal and in the permanent establishment of liberty of thought, of speech, of worship and of government will not, and must not, be permitted to weaken or to lose control of our mind and our action.

A little less than one hundred and fifty years ago this world was called upon to witness what may be described as a full dress rehearsal of that which is now going on. For nearly twenty years Napoleon Bonaparte dominated the continent of Europe and threatened Great Britain with invasion. He took over one government after another and put members of his family as puppets upon the thrones of kings and princes. He was apparently sweeping all before him when his unconquered ambition made the fatal mistake of invading distant Russia. That invasion proved to be the beginning of a final retreat. Discontent and dissatisfaction grew throughout the occupied territories of once independent nations. Then followed Waterloo, and Europe was set free again.

Today the world is awaiting another Waterloo. It may come on the continent of Europe, or it may come on the sea. It may come in Africa. It may come in Asia. We have faith that it will come. If and when this does come, let us make sure that our moral principles are so all-controlling, our courage so adequate and our foresight so clear, that the people of the United States and their government will take full responsibility for leadership in organizing the world of independent and liberal-minded nations. Only in this way can we re-establish prosperity and peace, to the end that the foundations upon which our life and government rest may never again be put in danger, and that no third Waterloo may ever be necessary.

XVII

MUST WE WAIT AND SEE?

An address delivered at the opening
of the 188th year of Columbia University
September 24, 1941

MUST WE WAIT AND SEE?

The highest type of ability in all which concerns the co-operation of men is what we call the administrative. Administration is the art of planning with foresight and of getting done with promptness, with effectiveness and at least possible cost of labor and of resources, all that represents and reflects the interests and ambitions of men in any given field of endeavor. History makes it very plain that from the earliest times there has been marked administrative ability in certain fields of human interest. Among these are the military, the ecclesiastical and the exploratory. Since the end of the eighteenth century, opportunities for the exercise of administrative ability have multiplied a thousandfold as a result of the industrial and economic evolution which has marked that period. In all that relates to production, to transportation, to commerce and to finance, administrative ability has found new opportunity in every part of the world and to an extent which would have seemed quite impossible a century and a half ago.

The most important field of human interest and co-operation in which administrative ability seems to lag is the governmental policies of the modern democracies. This was not always the case, as is made plain by a reading of the history of Great Britain in the seventeenth and eighteenth centuries, of France in the eighteenth century and of our own people when the foundations of our Federal Government were being laid and our political structure was being built upon those foundations. As the democratic process has developed and broadened, however, and as the number of individual citizens participating in the choice of political representatives and in the shaping of public policies has grown, differences of opinion and of personal and group interest have come to play a steadily increasing part in the story of governmental action. Theoretically, in each of these modern democracies, a majority rules. Theoretically, when a vote is taken on a very difficult and disputed matter and a clear majority is recorded in favor of one definite way of dealing with it, the chosen representatives of the people should at once and promptly act in accordance with what must be regarded as their instructions. But if the minority be cleverly led and armed with strong and persuasive arguments or supported by powerful emotion, there may be and there usually is indefinite delay in the formal action of public authority in respect to the matter under consideration. If, as so often happens when a general election of legislative representatives is held in a democracy, there are half a dozen questions at issue and not merely one question, then the problem presented to the legislative body grows in difficulty and in complexity. Under such circumstances, a first effort is usually to try to find a working hypothesis by which in one way or another all of the leading elements in the constituencies may be either satisfied or at least mollified. This of course does not make for efficiency or for good government. It makes simply for getting along in what appears to be the best way possible. It leaves unsettled

and unsolved numerous very important political problems, some of them quite fundamental. Just now there
are several such problems in our American political life,[1]
but there is no sign that the Government proposes to
take any action about them, simply because there are at
the moment no organized pressure groups armed with
political threats endeavoring to get action by the Federal
Government in regard to any one of them.

In such cases, the answer of the legislators is, Wait
and See. That has become a most popular slogan in all
the democracies. It has furnished and is furnishing material for sarcasm and for sneering at democracy by the
present-day despots and their blind followers. These
despots feel that they at least can get something done,
whether that something be military or civil, moral or
immoral, just or unjust, humane or cruel. They therefore claim for themselves and their doctrines a degree
of efficiency in administration which they insist the democracies cannot imitate and will not endeavor to imitate.

It must never be forgotten that in a democracy the
beginnings of all good government are to be found in
local self-government. It is in the community, be it
village or town, city or county, whose inhabitants are
immediately interdependent and closely in touch with
each other, that a high degree of efficiency in public administration usually exists. For example, in the United
States it is almost certain that the local police, the local
fire department and the local tax-supported schools are
effectively administered. When from these local politi-

[1]See Butler, Nicholas Murray, *Across the Busy Years* (New York:
Charles Scribner's Sons, 1939–40) II, 344–74.

cal units one moves to the government of a state or to that of the Federal Union, conditions sharply change. We then begin to find extravagance, duplication of organization and of effort, lack of effective oversight and in many ways lack of efficiency. An outstanding exception is the United States Postal Service, where there is a very high type of administrative efficiency. That service has the advantage of being very little and very infrequently interfered with by new forms of congressional action and control. It, therefore, can proceed on the basis of its own experience to serve the public with very high effectiveness in the field of communication, than which none is more important.

It is obvious that the policy of Wait and See will not do if democracy is to hold its own. Wait and See not only diminishes efficiency of governmental service, but it puts democracy itself in very great danger. In a world where every sort and kind of self-seeking is at work in order to control increasing numbers of human beings and widening areas of the earth's surface, a policy of Wait and See spells defeat. It should now be pretty plain that either this modern world is going to remain at war until the whole of what we call civilization has been destroyed and all its great monuments wrecked, or that the forces of constructive, liberal democracy will shortly be able to take leadership of the world and in reasonable time to put it upon a permanent foundation of order, of justice, of peace and of prosperity. This certainly cannot be done, however, by the policy of Wait and See. If we are only to Wait and See, then the believers in liberal democracy are openly handing control of the future to their bitter and determined enemies.

By great good fortune, mankind has just now been offered definite and specific leadership in its search for the foundations upon which to build a new and orderly world of prosperity and of peace. This is given by the Atlantic Declaration, announced to the world on August 14 last by the President of the United States of America and by the Prime Minister in the Government of Great Britain. To the American people, this Atlantic Declaration comes like a new Declaration of Independence in the field of national policy and international relations. It is supported with sympathy and understanding by those hopes and policies which have been close to the heart of the American people since the days of Washington and Franklin, of Hamilton and Jefferson. It echoes the famous sentence of President McKinley spoken forty years ago, "The period of exclusiveness is past." It is in harmony with the doctrines taught by President Theodore Roosevelt, Taft, Wilson and Harding, as well as with statements contained in the declarations of principle that were adopted by the Democrat National Convention and by the Republican National Convention of 1920. It is in accord with the instructions to the American delegates to the Hague Conference of 1907, given by Elihu Root, then Secretary of State. It is in accord with the Joint Resolution approved June 25, 1910, adopted without a dissenting vote by both Houses of the American Congress, calling for the limitation of armaments and for constituting the combined navies of the world an international police force for the preservation of universal peace.

This Atlantic Declaration, which in so complete and so splendid a fashion emphasizes and repeats this long series of statements of national policy, is the direct and conclusive answer to those who would continue to put their country in danger by preferring a policy of Wait and See. This is no time to Wait and See. The danger is too immediate and too great. It is time to Think and to Act.

XVIII

THE OUTLOOK FOR YOUTH

An address delivered to the
entering Freshman Class of Columbia College
McMillin Academic Theatre
October 7, 1941

THE OUTLOOK FOR YOUTH

Mr. Dean and the members of the incoming class in Columbia College: It is a great pleasure for me to have opportunity to stand face to face with you for a short time, to come to feel that I know you as a group, and to speak to you briefly of some of the things which it seems important for you to understand and to appreciate as you begin your college life.

Going to college is a turning point in the life of youth. For most collegians it means either going away from home or considerably changing the relationship with home because of the demands made upon time and thought by college association, college life and college work. Moreover, you have become members of a new society, new, that is, to you. However intimate and friendly you may have been with your companions in school, you now find you are entering into these friendly relationships with youths like yourself, drawn not only from every state in our Federal union, but from eight or ten countries in other parts of the world. In other words, you increase your common denominator of individual experience. The numerator remains yourself, your own personality, your own ambition, your own ability; but your common denominator has been enormously increased in power, in range, in interest and in influence.

It is important that you should fully appreciate what that common denominator means. It means, in the first place, coming under the influence of a great tradition. You have enrolled yourselves in an institution of higher learning which has now entered upon the one hundred and eighty-eighth year of its existence. It is one of the nine like institutions founded in the American Colonies before their independence and before the Government of the United States was established. Therefore it is one of those institutions with very noteworthy traditions of personal influence, personal distinction and personal service, going back now over nearly two hundred years.

To be a member of that society means very much, and it means, among other things, that you should quickly and without loss of opportunity come to some large and, if that be possible, complete comprehension of what that society means. It is important that you should get the stimulus, the comfort, the satisfaction and the pride which come from great traditions.

One of the first things which it is wise for you to do is to make inquiry as to who were those personalities whose noteworthy monuments stand about this campus. Who was Hamilton, for whom a Hall is named? Who was Livingston? Who was John Jay? Who was Schermerhorn? Who was Havemeyer? Who were these people? Why is it that they were thought important enough in our history and in the history of the nation to have buildings named for them? It is important for you to satisfy yourselves as to the answers to those questions because you now have become inheritors and participants in the great traditions which they represent.

One of the most striking things on this campus and

one which does not often attract public attention is the fact that it is the only place in America where there stand statues of Alexander Hamilton and of Thomas Jefferson. If you open the ordinary textbook of American history, you will find Hamilton and Jefferson recorded as violent opponents, as enemies, as representatives of conflicting views of the economic, social and political order. Why, then, are Hamilton, who was a graduate of old King's College, and Jefferson, who founded the University of Virginia, represented by these distinguished statues on South Field? The anwer is that if you will go down beneath the surface of American history, you will find these two men had more in common than they had in difference. They differed as to ways and means of accomplishing their ends, but for those ends they had like admiration and like conviction.

Hamilton, the greatest name in the history of Columbia, died at forty-seven, murdered in the duel with Aaron Burr. There are two events, incidents, in Hamilton's life which no Columbia man should forget. One is that when the Government was at its very beginning, when the capital was in Philadelphia, one evening, Alexander Hamilton and Thomas Jefferson walked together for two or three hours, backward and forward, in front of the house in which George Washington lived, discussing, first, where the capital of the nation should be, and, second, how the financial obligations of the new nation and its constituent states should be met. These two great leaders, profound political philosophers, differing, I repeat, when viewed superficially, as to methods of proceeding, were one in believing that those two problems must quickly be solved. They were solved in the way which Hamilton suggested, and the District of Columbia was set up and in it was put the capital of the nation, named for its first President.

The second incident is this. After Hamilton left the Treasury, he came back to New York and engaged in the practice of law. He lived in a little house on what is now about 68 Wall Street. One night, when the great French politician and philosopher Talleyrand was in this country, he was walking up Wall Street with a friend, and they passed the house in which Hamilton lived. They stopped. It was summer. The weather was warm. The window was open; and there, clearly to be seen from the sidewalk, was Alexander Hamilton working over his law books under an oil lamp. Talleyrand stopped and turned to his friend. He said, "My friend, there is the eighth wonder of the world. There is a man who has created a nation working at night for the support of his family." It was a great tribute to Talleyrand's insight and skill that he saw what Hamilton meant for our country and for the world and was enabled to interpret it.

And so if you go down through our list of great names, all the way down to our great scholars—I omit those of today naturally—of the generation recently closed, you will find name after name that will give you a thrill of pride and satisfaction when you say, "I am a member of the same college in which he taught; I am a member of the same college in which he was a student."

First of all, get the point of view of membership in this historic intellectual family which has meant so much for the American people through all these years, and then remember that what you have come to college to get is the foundation of a liberal education. You have not come to college primarily to be trained to earn a living, although earning a living will be aided by what you do here. Primarily your task is to get a liberal education. Under the leadership of Dean Hawkes and the admirable College faculty which will supervise and direct your work, the Columbia College of today has arrived at an answer to the question, "What is a liberal education?" which to my mind is the best answer to that question that any American college has been able to make.

In my college days, all studies were prescribed. We all took precisely the same subjects at precisely the same hours. I think there were one or two alternatives in the senior year, but that was all. This was because the faculty of that day believed that we would thus get the best training for life. But the trouble was that the subjects chosen were inherited from a hundred years before and took no account of the new subjects which had come into existence through the discoveries of modern science, through the building up of economics and the branches of knowledge growing out of it, and of the widening of the meaning of the word "literature." Therefore it was found that students of my time, while getting what had been a satisfactory foundation of a liberal education, were going out of college without contact with a great many subjects of which they should know something.

That fact led to the movement for the elective system, and we soon began to hear, "Let students take what they want; do not prescribe that they should take anything." The consequence was that in fifteen or twenty years the whole conception of liberal education had broken down and nobody was getting a liberal education of any kind. The record of scholarship of that period proves how unfortunate were the results.

Then the Columbia faculty addressed itself to the question of solving the problem of a liberal education, without ultra-prescription, in terms of today. They brought into existence some years ago those very extraordinary courses in contemporary civilization, in modern science, and in the liberal arts, which you will all take and which will give you in concentrated and compressed form the elements, historic and traditional, of a liberal education as it is understood today.

I regard the work of the dean and faculty in directing and organizing those courses as of the very first order of importance. It is a great satisfaction to know that they are being imitated, in one form or another, in other parts of the country. The reason is that they represent a real solution of a very real and a very difficult problem.

If you are taking fifteen or sixteen hours of study a week, if each one of those hours is prescribed for four years, you cannot possibly get in contact with all the elements of knowledge that you naturally desire. If, on the other hand, you take only those things which appeal at the moment to your imagination and your interest, without guidance and without counsel, then in nine cases out of ten, the essentials of a liberal education will not be given at all, and your years in College will be largely wasted. You are very fortunate, you members of this incoming class, in coming into a college where that problem has progressed so far toward a satisfactory and a convincing solution.

Wholly apart from your work in the College, you are

face to face with quite the most amazing world which history records. We may read, as we do, of the extraordinary happenings of civilizations gone by, of centuries that have passed, of generations that are dead; but never has there been anything written in history comparable to what is going on today. That which is going on is, to the amazement of so many of us, the most violent form of reaction. If it were progress, even unwise progress, we might wish to know more of it and to see whether it could not have some of our sympathy; but when we see pure and simple reaction, when we see the standards of morality, of religious faith, of civil liberty destroyed, not only destroyed but scoffed at, and when we are told that the fundamental principles of civilization which we supposed were conquering the world, slowly perhaps, and on which our own Government was based more than one hundred and fifty years ago—when we are told that those principles no longer exist, that nobody is going to accept them any more, that there is just one rule, brute force, seeking world domination—then, as youths, you are face to face with reaction to barbarism of the most extreme type.

Some of us of the older generation are staggered by it. You may not be staggered at first because you have not and cannot have the insight into what had been and what had been going forward which characterizes the experience and the knowledge of older men. But one object of your liberal education will be to enable you to face those happenings with open mind, with even mind, with clearness of thought, with true vision, and, as the years pass, to take your part in leading the world forward to a path of progress either on the old lines or on new lines of progress that may be still wiser and still more hopeful.

You are going to be confronted by some very extraordinary states of mind and policy. You are going to be confronted by persecution, persecution which is hailed and cheered and extolled as desirable. It is persecution in various forms.

One of its forms is persecution of the successful. That is the outcome of envy, hatred and malice. He who has been successful must, we are told, have been successful not because of ability, not because of the use of opportunity, but because of some advantage or privilege concealed from the public which somehow or other he acquired and used for his own gain and to the disadvantage of all of his fellow men. That doctrine has been preached now for one hundred years. It is losing its popularity because its essential falsity is becoming increasingly clear.

Then we have, to our amazement, religious and racial persecution. We are told in some of these countries given over to the so-called New Order—the oldest order that history records!—that not only may they not have freedom of religion, but no religion at all; their churches must be closed, if necessary burned, because loyalty to a form of faith is at war with loyalty to the ruling dictator. It involves possible, almost certain, contradiction, and therefore this form of loyalty to religious faith or principle or to a ruling group must be forbidden in the interest of the dictatorship itself.

That has taken a form which is perfectly amazing, even in countries where religion had been free for two hundred or three hundred years, and it has staggered men and women all over the world.

We also see racial persecution, quite extraordinary in its extent and in its bitterness. Sometimes it is combined with religious persecution, sometimes it is apart from that. It is of vital importance that American youth seeking a liberal education should hold themselves above and out of reach of all that sort of thing.

In this country we have had in recent years, and we have now, in extraordinary fashion, racial persecution combined with religious persecution. The Ku Klux Klan persecution of members of the Catholic Church has lost a great deal of its vigor, but it still exists among certain classes of the community. The violence which attached to it, for example, in the presidential campaign of 1928, when one of the candidates for the presidency was a member of the Roman Catholic Church, will not soon be forgotten by those of us who were so appalled by it. But it has lost a great deal of its force, and it is sincerely to be hoped that it will depart and never return to our American life.

The anti-Semitic persecution is different. That has had not a world-wide, but a many-nationed basis for a long time. It has not been serious until recently in France, and it has not been serious in Great Britain. It has become of the utmost violence in Italy and in Germany under the present dictatorships.

When you remember how few Jews there are in Italy and how relatively few there are in Germany, one must wonder at the violence and the bitterness of this persecution. The number of Jews in Italy is only a small fraction of those in the city of New York, while there are in the city of New York six times as many Jews as there were in the German Reich when the last war ended and possibly more than four times as many as there are there now. Yet the persecution, personal, physical, family, financial, goes on, openly and secretly, in a way that is perfectly appalling. To my great astonishment, this anti-Semitic persecution has been violently and publicly revived in this country within the last few weeks or months, and it is as discreditable to us that this should have happened as anything that we can imagine.

Jews differ among themselves just as do Spaniards or Italians or Canadians or Americans. There are some who belong to one party, some who belong to another; some who hold one point of view, some who hold a point of view that is contradictory. The notion that all who belong to that race or profess that faith are of one mind in everything that relates to their public relationships is a grotesque departure from fact. But if you can play upon an excited public emotion by the use of these terms and by the insinuation that the entire Hebrew population is engaged, let us say—as we have been told from the platform recently—in trying to get this nation into war, such statements, although absolutely contradictory to every well-known fact, will, if repeated long enough, be believed and acted upon by a certain number of our unthinking population.

We cannot protest too vigorously and too strongly against that sort of thing. It may be the Ku Klux Klan persecuting the Catholics; it may be the anti-Semites persecuting the Jews: but persecution on racial or religious ground has absolutely no place in a nation given over to liberty and which calls itself a democracy.

Let me remind you that you have come into a college which is very proud of the outstanding Jews who have been carried upon its rolls in years past. At the close of the eighteenth century one of its most distinguished and useful Trustees was the truly great Rabbi Seixas, who, by the way, was the first rabbi to preach in English in a Hebrew synagogue. He played a very large part in the intellectual life of New York, and he played a very effective part in the guidance and development of old Columbia College. We then had Doctor Joseph, also at the close of that century, a student of medicine, who devoted himself to trying to protect the public from the great yellow-fever epidemic of 1798, but who, despite his efforts, unfortunately lost his own life in it. Then there was Jonathan Nathan, of the Class of 1827, a fellow classmate of Hamilton Fish, Secretary of State of the United States for eight years. The correspondence between Nathan and Fish, covering every type of interest and public service, is fortunately in the possession of this university and is a source of the greatest significance for the history of the United States.

And then in our own time we have had the two great men, Edwin Seligman, of the Class of 1879, outstanding economist of the last generation, and Benjamin N. Cardozo, of the Class of 1889, than whom no one ranks higher in the juristic history of the United States.

We point to these men and we say, when you are called upon to enter upon a racial or a religious persecution, please stop long enough to see what the history of Columbia has to say about men of that faith or of that race. It might at any moment occur to some of those who use this mode of approach to human emotion to pass from the Roman Catholic and the Jew and to take up some other form of faith or belief and to circulate the report underground that it was in violent opposition to American ideals and American principles.

No, young men, you are living at a time when, being in search of a liberal education, you must keep your eyes open, your heart and head clear, and stop to think. Do not be swept off your feet by phrases or words or torrential eloquence. Ask, What lies behind it all? What are the observable, the measurable, the justifiable facts? And then upon those facts build your own convictions and shape your own lives.

My hope, my faith is that out of this splendid group gathered here this afternoon, Columbia will recruit another regiment of young Americans to go out into the world and fight the battle for American principles in the field of intellect, in the field of morals, in the field of public service. May success and happiness attend you each and all.

XIX

THE DUTY OF FREE PEOPLES
NEW YEAR'S MESSAGE, 1942

A message broadcast by transcription
to Australia over the International
Short-wave Radio, January 5, 1942

THE DUTY OF FREE PEOPLES
NEW YEAR'S MESSAGE, 1942

No answer has yet been given to the questions which were pressed upon public opinion by my New Year's Day Message of 1941. It was then asked what cause could be given for the gigantic collapse of the rule of intelligence, of morals and of law upon which the world had been looking. During 1941 that collapse has become more complete and more appalling, but the questions as to what may be its cause remain unanswered.

At the moment, the whole world is to all intents and purposes at war. By far the greater part of it is engaged in declared military war. Those few peoples who are not so engaged are subject to economic attack and political undermining and may at any moment find themselves forced into the military war which rages all around the globe. Some of the unprovoked attacks by Nazis on eastern European nations were surely bad enough, but all these were far outdone by the utterly shocking behavior of the government of Japan in its naval and air attack on Pearl Harbor while a special ambassador and his technical advisers were at Washington to urge upon the President and the Secretary of State farther prolongation of the consideration and discussion of the bases of a possible peace in the Pacific. This happening outranks all others in immorality and in perfidy. It calls for, and is certain to receive, the most complete and drastic punishment.

The democratic peoples are paying the penalty of their belief that governments with whom they had made agreements were telling the truth; that the Pact of Paris renouncing war as an instrument of national policy meant what it said; and that international co-operation to lay new and stronger foundations for a world of prosperity and peace would shortly be well under way. Every one of these assumptions proved to be contrary to plainly observed and now definitely recorded facts. Therefore it is immorality which is ruling the world at the moment and inflicting upon civilization by far the severest blow which it has ever received. Not only are non-combatant human beings, men, women and children, being killed, injured and starved by the hundreds of thousands, but the earnings and savings of civilized nations for centuries are being poured out in wasteful and murderous attacks upon fellow men. Great cathedrals and churches, noteworthy libraries, museums and art galleries, and public buildings of beauty as well as of great historic importance are destroyed with as much carelessness and completeness as though they were forts and air bases with military value.

There is no escape from the conclusion that the free peoples who believe in a prosperous and peaceful world of co-operating nations must make that belief possible and practicable by bending every energy to bring this military contest to an early and complete victory. There is no use in talking of peace when murder is being committed in your presence. If there is to be peace, there must be in control of the world's policies those who believe in peace, who will establish peace and who will defend peace.

No community has yet become so civilized and so highly moral that it can dispense with police and fire-men. Obviously this world will for a long time need its international police and its international firemen in order that the lofty ideals in which the friends and expounders of liberty believe may be achieved, well established and protected. To refuse to defend liberty is to surrender to cruel and murderous despotism.

Public opinion in the United States must grasp these facts and act in accordance with them. That public opinion must fix its eyes on post-war conditions and be prepared to take the leadership which history has put in the hands of the people of the United States to aid the world in doing for itself what the people of the United States and those of the British Commonwealth of Nations found a way to do for themselves. The path to this end may not be short, but it can be clearly marked and defined, and the American people must prepare themselves to travel on it for generations to come. The English, the American and the French revolutions are dominating chapters in the history of the modern liberal movement. The reactionary movement, now so power-fully armed and so desperately manifested, must be promptly met and overturned in order that the march of liberalism may be resumed not only by and for the peoples of the British Commonwealth of Nations, of the United States of America and of France, but for every other people, great or small, which has in all reason and truth the right to an independent and a self-controlled life and government. To end war, the civilized world must unite to control and remove the causes of war.

May the people of Australia remain forever free and independent as members of the truly great British Commonwealth of Nations. The principles upon which that Commonwealth is built may well prove to point the way to a successful organization of all nations, great and small, to establish and protect prosperity and peace.

XX

THERE CAN BE NO ISOLATION

An address delivered at the Annual Meeting
of the Pilgrims of the United States
The Bankers Club, New York
January 28, 1942

THERE CAN BE NO ISOLATION

When the nineteenth century was coming to its end, Prince Bismarck, who had lived through more than eighty of its years, was asked what he considered to have been its chief characteristic. He answered, "The fact that the North American nations speak the English language."

That was the answer of a statesman who was also a philosopher. Bismarck foresaw that as the Victorian era came to its end, a new series of social, economic and political problems were to confront the world, and that the center of gravity of the Western World was to cross the Atlantic. He foresaw that the English language would be the controlling and shaping influence of the progressive human spirit in attempting the solution of these new and far-reaching problems.

We do not stop to think, as we should, of the significance of language. A language is something much more than a mode of speech. It is a vehicle of experience and of achievement, of likes and of dislikes, of prejudices and of affections, of ideas and of ideals. One has only to look back at the Latin language of the ancient Romans, which controlled southern and western Europe for eight hundred years, to see how completely a language carries with it the point of view, the experience, the ideals, of those whose language it is. When the time came for the centralized power of that language to break down and it was succeeded by languages Latin in base—the Italian, the French, the Spanish and the Portuguese—another chapter of the history of Europe began to be written in terms of the likenesses and the differences of those languages.

Meanwhile, in the northwest of Europe, the English language had been forming, chiefly from a Teuton root. Cut off from the rest of the world by the waters which surrounded the British Isles, it began speedily to take on its own individuality, to write its own literature, to develop its own reflective thought and to make its own contributions to history.

From the day of Magna Carta—the title of which is Latin, but the spirit and content of which are English— to the present day, that English language has become increasingly the organ of the advancing liberal, constructive outlook and spirit which have been marked by great historic events, one after the other, in the English-speaking nations.

Nothing is more extraordinary than the way in which the English language has, on this side of the Atlantic, conquered one stream of immigration after another, taken the place of its native language, and in very large part dispossessed the ideas and points of view with which those streams of immigrants came to this country. It substituted for them the outlook, the experience and the point of view which are those of the English language and of those who habitually use it.

It so happens that the English-speaking peoples have been, practically from the beginning, peoples of world-wide interest and world-wide influence. The Portuguese and the Spanish set out to explore and to settle distant parts of the world. Their achievements and their results, important though they were for the time being, fall far short of those of Great Britain and the English-speaking peoples. The English language is now heard in every quarter of the globe. The characteristics which it reflects and represents are well-known and clearly understood, and as a result their conquering power grows almost day by day.

There is a curious superstition, repeated from time to time—with frequency just now—in the public press and on the floor of the Congress of the United States, that the traditional policy of the Americans is one of isolation from world affairs. That statement is flatly contradicted by one great series of events after another from the time this country was first settled. No people except the English themselves have ever been so completely and so constantly interested in world affairs, whether economic, social or political, and so eager to take some part in shaping them, as has the American people. We began long, long ago when William Penn founded the colony which was to become the State of Pennsylvania. He then brought forward the first plan for international organization to establish world peace. How many remember that Benjamin Franklin, ten years before the Declaration of Independence, was summoned to appear before the House of Commons and was cross-examined at length as to why it was that the Amercian Colonies would not accept the Stamp Act, a form of taxation imposed upon them by the British Parliament? He presented in that testimony, recorded word for word in the minutes of Parliament, the argument for national independence and international co-operation. Remember, too, the Olive Branch Petition, after Lexington, Concord and Bunker Hill! That Petition, signed by the very men who nine months afterward signed the Declaration of Independence, was sent to the King proposing the precise relation between the American Colonies and the Crown which Canada and Australia occupy today. And that was in 1775. Remember that Thomas Jefferson, the author of the Declaration of Independence, sat in Paris when the Constituent Assembly was formulating its Declaration of the Rights of Man. They invited Jefferson to sit with them formally. He replied that he was not a Frenchman, but an American, and that it would not be becoming for him to take formal part in drafting such a document. However, he met with them time after time and hour after hour, and as a result the Declaration of Independence and the Bill of Rights of the Federal Constitution are, in spirit, written into the French Declaration of the Rights of Man. Not long afterward, John Adams, in London and in Paris, interpreted the new American form of government to the English and the French with surprising clearness and emphasis. John Marshall, afterward Chief Justice of the United States, did the same thing during his brief service in France. Then there is the oft-quoted and much misinterpreted statement made by Thomas Jefferson in his first inaugural address: "Peace, commerce and honest friendship with all nations—entangling alliances with none." It was Thomas Jefferson, also, who insisted upon the duty of the American government to protect the freedom of the seas from the Barbary pirates.

How many of us remember three of the greatest

speeches ever made in the House of Representatives of the American Congress which illustrate the interest of our great leaders of opinion and thought in international happenings and international relations? Daniel Webster, Representative in Congress from the State of New Hampshire, delivered a most vigorous and violent attack upon the War of 1812, which he denounced as absolutely unnecessary and as against the interest of the American people. He was in a minority at the time, but when the Treaty of Ghent was signed three years later, it contained no mention, direct or indirect, of the alleged causes of that war.

Shortly thereafter came the epoch-marking speech of Henry Clay, Representative in Congress from the State of Kentucky—the speech which called the Latin-American republics into existence and led to their recognition by the nations of Europe. So powerful, so convincing and so influential was that speech that ten or fifteen years afterward Richard Rush wrote to Clay saying that he and he alone was responsible for the creation of the Latin-American republics.

Abraham Lincoln, Representative in Congress from the State of Illinois, voted against the war with Mexico and delivered a most convincing speech attacking the Government for having entered upon that war unconstitutionally and without reason.

Remember, too, that it was Commodore Perry of the United States Navy who, to all intents and purposes, discovered Japan and opened the ports of that nation to the trade of the world.

Then we come from one great event to another, until we find ourselves confronted by the influence of that policy of economic nationalism which, however apparently beneficial in its immediate results, leads sooner or later to what this one led—the great depression which began in 1929, and those feuds between nations based upon economic ambition which are rocking the world today.

There was new hope and new promise when President McKinley struck the note which he did in the remarkable address made the day before he fell by the hand of an assassin. A few years later his successor in office, Theodore Roosevelt, having left the presidency, made an important speech at Christiana in accepting the Nobel peace prize. He outlined and strongly endorsed the plan for international organization to protect the world's peace in the form which came before the world in a very few years.

Hardly any American—apparently no one now in Congress—realizes that in June, 1910, nearly thirty-two years ago, the Congress by the unanimous vote of both Houses called upon the President to invite the nations of the world to organize for the establishment of international peace, to be protected by an international police force made up of the combined navies of the world. There was not a dissenting vote, Republican or Democrat, in the Senate or House of Representatives.

Then came the vision of Woodrow Wilson, the history of which we all know. But we do not remember the speech made by Warren G. Harding toward the close of his campaign for the presidency in 1920. He then said:

The other type is a society of free nations, or an association of free nations, or a league of free nations, animated by considerations of right and justice, instead of might and self-interest, and not merely proclaimed an agency in pursuit of peace, but so organized and so participated in as to make the actual attainment of peace a reasonable possibility. Such an association I favor with all my heart, and I would make no fine distinction as to whom credit is due. One need not care what it is called. Let it be an association, a society, or a league, or what not, our concern is solely with the substance, not the form thereof.

The platforms of both great American political parties in 1920, 1924, 1928 and 1932, endorsed American participation and leadership in the movement for world organization to secure prosperity and peace upon foundations of justice and liberal political philosophy.

Where has this notion of a traditional international isolation come from? It is invented by those who have no conception of the facts of our history or of the statements of our outstanding leaders. That isolation which they thought so admirable because it was protected by thousands of miles of ocean and of air, they now find to be made impossible by the two best-paved roads in the world—the ocean and the air. There are no roads in existence over which traffic or attack can be so sudden, so complete or, in many ways, so safe. As a matter of fact, the policy of isolation, which professes to avoid war and to seek peace, invites unwilling participation in every war of importance which may break out anywhere in the world. It invites that participation with the assurance of defeat, through lack of foresight or preparation for national defense. It is a policy of smug complacency.

It is time for us to face the facts—to face the responsibility which rests upon all the English-speaking peoples and which is now being borne in upon us with convincing force by the happenings of the past few weeks. It is a far cry in years from Magna Carta of 1215 to the Atlantic Charter of 1941, but the steps from the one to the other are steady, continuous and unbroken.

We have seen the stirring spectacle of the Prime Minister of the Government of Great Britain as a guest at the White House and standing in person before the Congress of the United States and before the Parliament of the Dominion of Canada. Those acts of themselves are significant and revealing of the personal relationships which underlie and accompany the consciousness of common responsibility, common ideals, and joint and common power which rests upon our English-speaking peoples. We are looking forward—not to one generation or to one century—we are looking forward to a period which may be as long in time as the rule of ancient Rome, and in which those ideals of free and liberal democracy may be guaranteed to every nation, great or small, living in a world of peace and friendly economic relationships. It will go down into history a thousand years from now, and men will look back upon it just as we look back upon the rule of the Romans.

Remember that the ocean which once separated Great Britain and the United States, the United States and Australia, now joins them together. Remember that in Great Britain, in Canada, in the United States and in Australia, these fundamental facts are being grasped day by day by public opinion. When this dreadful attack upon all forms of mental, moral and political progress shall have been resisted and broken, then the English-speaking peoples, regardless of their apparent separation by ocean or by air, will be called upon to go forward as the leaders in those constructive policies upon which alone a new, a peaceful, a prosperous and a moral world can rise.

INDEX

INDEX

233

A

Date Due
